fRAGmentation

The Power of e Pluribus Unum

Alex Bennet
Mountain Quest Institute

FIRST EDITION (Softback)

MQIPress
Frost, West Virginia
303 Mountain Quest Lane, Marlinton, WV 24954
United States of America
Telephone: 304-799-7267
eMail: alex@mountainquestinstitute.com
www.mqresearchcenter.com
www.mountainquestinn.com

ISBN 978-1-949829-88-4

Fragmentation [French or Latin *fragmentum* from base of *frangere* break] The action of breaking or separating into fragments; in BIOLOGY separation into parts which form new individuals or units.

Coherence [Latin *cohaerentia* formed as next] 1. The action or fact of sticking together. 2. Logical or clear interconnection or relation; consistency; congruity of substance, tenor, or general effect. B. Coincidence, agreement. 3. Context; immediately surrounding discourse. 4. PHYSICS The property (of waveforms) of being coherent.

Shorter Oxford English Dictionary (Fifth Edition)

Fragmentation herein is expanded to a new level of understanding and appreciation for related principles and processes that function in both the natural and constructed world domains. Selected examples of fragmentation inform and illuminate. In addition, we share increasing awareness of how fragmentation underpins the development of civilization and is a harbinger of the transformation of humankind.

Dedication

As the natural and constructed world tears itself apart, with so many choosing to leave and others struggling to redefine meaning and purpose, this book emerges from the chaos to bring hope for the future. It is in our hands, minds, hearts and souls. This book is for you.

Appreciation *to Dr. Annie Green, Mountain Quest Institute Associate, for her close read and feedback. Appreciation of AI-PRO 4o for scenario assistance and DALL-E for visual aids.*

Preface

As the concept of fRAGmentation kept waking me and pushing my thought toward the keyboard, I began to recognize the need for greater understanding and deeper reflection in this area. Then when my friend and colleague Robert Turner was here with his wife Jane for my son's wedding, he read some of these early thoughts and asked: "Is it entropy or perturbation?" More reflection. And so began the quest for understanding the challenges and opportunities offered in this age of fragmentation.

Indeed, fragmentation can be considered both in terms of entropy and perturbation. In the general sense, entropy refers to the level of disorder or randomness in a system. If you consider fragmentation as a process that increases the disorder of a system, like breaking a solid piece into smaller, scattered parts, then it can be associated with entropy. This is often related to the idea that systems tend to move towards a state of higher entropy over time, leading to more randomness and less order.

In the grand experiment with the American civilization, fragmentation was anticipated and carefully regarded. From July 4, 1776, we have the original theme of the new union *e pluribus unum* (13 letters representing the 13 colonies), "out of many, one", reflecting the idea of unity within diversity. To be sure, the principal designers—Adams, Franklin, Hamilton, Jay, Jefferson, Madison, and Washington—drew upon the philosophers—Hobbes, Locke, Montesquieu and Rousseau—and reached beyond the organizing of the individual colonies as an entity. They envisioned the formidable bonding of all citizen contributions and in the integral integrity of the richness of that vibrant union a powerful culture and system of governance was created with a balance of fostering freedom and sustaining the rule of law as a check and balance.

Some years ago, in this century, a seasoned member of the U.S. federal judiciary reflected to one of the authors that the brilliance of the American Constitution was largely in how it did not unduly impose limitations. To be sure, fragmentation was not only expected, it was respected. Concomitantly, in the infinite diversity in the natural world, we enjoy Earth as the preeminent ecosystem in our known universe. Likewise, out of the collective regard for all humanity, we prosper in the synergy of democracy. As the founders understood this, they created a form of governance with the supporting Charters of Freedom that creates a crescendo of fragmentation. Evidence of the brilliance of American democracy is the proliferation of democracies throughout the world in over 80 nations as reported by Freedom House at and the use of the American Constitution as a valued reference for the writing of constitutions across the world. [*Reference: See* www.freedomhouse.org]

On the other hand, advanced perturbation theory refers to changes in a complex system that create a new overall capacity to function—essentially a state change. Generally, in perturbation theory one identifies the solution to a similar problem and replicates the solution applied in that instance. Understanding the fragmentation issues and options in the former solution is key to replication of results. So, the solution depends on identifying which set of critical nodes of fragmentation to focus on. If it's about focusing on particular functions of a system, it's more about entropy. If it's about a considerable change in the performance of a system, it's about perturbation. In his work with systems, Novel Prize winning physicist Ilya Prigogine offered that the selection of an optimum set of critical nodes would yield state change. [*Reference:* Prigogine, I., & Stenger, I. (2017). *Order Out of Chaos: Man's New Dialogues with Nature.* Verso.]

Alvin Toeffler, the noted historian, in his in depth and insightful foreword to *Order Out of Chaos* closes with: *It projects science into today's revolution world of instability, disequilibrium, and turbulence. In so doing, it serves the highest creative function—it helps us create fresh order.*

From a broad perspective, there is no doubt that the world exhibits characteristics of fragmentation. There are numerous areas where divisions and disconnects are evidence, such as in social, economic, political, and environmental contexts. Many societies are grappling with deep-seated issues like political polarization, economic disparities, and cultural tensions, which often result in fragmented communities and nations.

Conflicts and disagreements among countries further contribute to a fragmented global landscape, making it challenging to address transnational issues like climate change and humanitarian crises effectively. In addition, the rise of digital technology and social media has both connected and divided people, sometimes exacerbating divisions by fostering echo chambers and misinformation.

Simultaneously, there's also a significant push toward unity and collaboration. Efforts to address global issues through international organizations, grassroots movements aimed at social justice, and widespread calls for environmental sustainability reflect a desire to overcome these fragmentations despite the current disruptive and fragmenting actions of the United States government. So, while fragmentation is a prominent feature of today's world, it's important to recognize the counter-movements striving for greater cohesion and cooperation. The dynamics between these opposing tendencies shape much of the global discourse and action in our time

Fragmentation can also be seen as a paradox. The paradox of fragmentation lies in its dual nature of being both detrimental and beneficial, depending on the context and perspective. On one hand, fragmentation is often viewed negatively because it can lead to inefficiencies, loss of cohesion, and increased disorder within a system. For instance, in ecological habitats, fragmentation can disrupt ecosystems and reduce biodiversity, making it harder for species to survive. In the digital realm, fragmented files on a computer can slow down access times and reduce overall performance.

On the other hand, fragmentation, as we are presenting it, can also be seen as a positive force. It can stimulate innovation and adaptation by breaking down monolithic structures and encouraging diversity. In economic and business contexts, the fragmentation of large monopolies can open up the market for smaller players, fostering competition and leading to better services or products. In biology, genetic fragmentation through mutations can drive evolution, allowing species to adapt to changing environments.

Thus, the paradox of fragmentation is rooted in its ability to simultaneously challenge and stimulate systems, highlighting the complexity and multifaceted nature of change within any given context. This dual role serves as a reminder that fragmentation, while often disruptive, can also be a catalyst for transformation and growth.

We explore this dual nature through the lens of five domains of fragmentation: physical, holistic human, digital, narrative/art, and societal. And, as we expand our understanding, we will embrace societal political fragmentation—at the forefront in today's chaotic world—as a core focus, offering us depth of fodder to explore this important area and the role individually and collectively that we can play in the unfolding challenges of societal fragmentation.

We begin.

Alex Bennet

Contents

Foreword

The world is silently fragmenting, yet the echoes resonate in every corner of our lives, leaving us to navigate through pieces that no longer fit together as they once did.

As you journey through this book, remember that YOU are not a passive observer but an active participant. YOU are the expert on the fragmentation in your own life, uniquely positioned to connect the broader themes discussed here with your personal experiences. YOU are the expert that is writing this Foreword, and the Afterword.

This is an invitation to delve deep, challenge assumptions, and explore the intersections between the external world and your inner landscape. Our journey into wholeness begins now as we explore that landscape.

1. **What aspects of your life feel fragmented right now?**

2. **How does the fragmentation around you reflect in your personal circumstances and community?**

3. **In what ways are reductions in support and safety systems, like government benefits, affecting your stability?**

4. **Where in your life do you see possibilities for healing and rebuilding?**

5. **What actions can you take to navigate or mend the fragmented pieces in your life?**

As you reflect on these questions, consider them as starting points for a deeper exploration of how fragmentation affects various aspects of your life and the world. Throughout this book, you'll gain insights and tools to better understand and navigate these complexities, ultimately empowering you to foster connection and resilience in your personal and global communities. These reflections are your guideposts. Allow yourself to engage deeply, drawing strength from your own stories, as together we explore the paths towards more cohesive and harmonious living. And as you move through this thought, ask and reflect: "How do I envision my role as a connector or bridge-builder in a fragmented world?"

/s/ YOU, THE EXPERT

Chapter 1
The Shattered World

In the heart of a lush valley, lay the once-united village of Eldoria. Surrounded by emerald hills and a river that shimmered under the sun, Eldoria was a tight-knit community where families had lived for generations, their lives intertwined like the roots of the ancient oak at the village center.

But over time, things changed. A mining company discovered precious minerals beneath the village's fertile land. Contracts were signed, and soon, the landscape transformed as machinery carved deep scars into the earth.

As the physical landscape fractured, so did the community. The river that once flowed freely was now diverted, splitting the village in two. The northern half struggled to access clean water, while those in the south prospered as they sold their land to the company.

This physical divide deepened social rifts. Friendships crumbled as debates over the mine's impact turned neighbors into adversaries. Families were torn apart, choosing sides based on immediate needs versus long-term vision. The school, previously a bustling hub of learning and laughter, sat half-empty as families were forced to leave for opportunities elsewhere.

Eldoria, once a symbol of unity and resilience, became a living testament to fragmentation. The walls of division, though invisible, were felt by every person still living in the shadow of the mine.

This story of Eldoria is not unique. Across the globe, fragmentation is a growing force, affecting communities, economies, and even entire nations. As we explore the dynamics of fragmentation, we begin to understand how interconnected these divides truly are and what it takes to mend them.

This is our world, a tapestry woven with threads of diversity and division. And like so many places around the globe, Eldoria became a victim of fragmentation. Yet, the deepest divisions were not of earth and rock, but of soul and spirit. The river that cradled Eldoria now separated more than it connected, its diverted waters mirroring the diverging paths of its people. In place of shared hopes, debates fierce and bitter took root, growing into walls that kept neighbors apart. Those who once shared markets and meals drifted into camps of 'us' versus 'them'—a fracture far harder to mend than topography.

Eldoria is a microcosm of our world today, where the push and pull between sustainable development and the preservation of community traditions, the intricate dance of wealth and equitable distribution fostering collective well-being, and the critical balance between power, accountability, and democratic participation converge. These dynamics reflect the broader challenges we face globally, as we strive to create harmonious societies that honor both progress and heritage. Perhaps through Eldoria's fractured past, we can explore the universal themes of fragmentation, understand their complex causes, and seek the shared paths toward healing and unity that can redefine our future.

Global Challenges

Across nations, *economic disparities*, the stark divide between the affluent and the impoverished, continues to widen, posing significant threats to societal cohesion and economic stability. Global economic inequality remains a pressing challenge, with wealth concentrated in the hands of a few while vast numbers of people struggle to make ends meet. This imbalance not only affects individual well-being but also poses significant risks to global stability and peace. The growing gap exacerbates social tensions and can lead to unrest and conflict, as those left behind demand fairness and justice. Addressing economic disparities requires concerted efforts in policy-making, investment in education and skills development, and innovative approaches to wealth distribution and opportunity creation.

In an increasingly interconnected world, *global health challenges* underscore the urgent need for resilient healthcare systems and international collaboration to protect public well-being. The COVID-19 pandemic has laid bare the vulnerabilities in global health systems, highlighting the need for robust healthcare infrastructure and international collaboration. Beyond pandemics, we face ongoing challenges with infectious diseases, mental health, and access to basic healthcare services. Addressing global health issues requires a comprehensive approach that includes strengthening healthcare systems, increasing funding for research and development, and enhancing preparedness for future health crises. Collaboration and knowledge-sharing across borders are essential in building resilient health systems that can protect us all

The planet faces a critical juncture, as the urgent need for *environmental sustainability* clashes with traditional growth models, demanding innovative solutions and global cooperation. Climate change and environmental degradation are among the most urgent issues facing our world today. Rising temperatures, extreme weather events, and loss of biodiversity threaten ecosystems and human societies alike. Nations struggle with the transition to sustainable energy sources while balancing economic growth. The challenge is compounded by the need for international cooperation and commitment, as environmental issues transcend borders. To mitigate these impacts, global efforts must focus on reducing carbon emissions, protecting natural habitats, and fostering sustainable practices among businesses and communities.

The world is witnessing unprecedented *migration and refugee movements*, driven by war, persecution, and environmental disasters, presenting profound humanitarian and logistical challenges. Wars, persecution, and natural disasters have displaced millions, leading to unprecedented levels of migration and refugee crises. These movements pose challenges for both origin and destination countries, impacting social services and infrastructure. Addressing these issues involves not only providing immediate humanitarian assistance but also implementing long-term solutions that integrate displaced populations into host communities and address root causes.

As *climate change and population growth* exert pressure on natural resources, ensuring food security and managing water scarcity have become paramount global concerns. Ensuring access to sufficient, safe, and nutritious food is a growing concern as the global population increases and climate change impacts agricultural systems. Water scarcity, exacerbated by climate change and overuse, further threatens food production and human populations. Efforts to enhance sustainable agriculture, improve water management, and reduce waste are critical to addressing these intertwined challenges.

In many regions around the globe, the shadows of *political instability and conflict* loom large, disrupting lives and repeating history, undermining the prospects for peace and progress. Geopolitical tensions and internal conflicts continue to pose critical challenges worldwide. Political instability can lead to humanitarian crises, disrupt economies, and prevent the effective governance needed to address other global issues. Efforts toward diplomatic resolution, peace-building, and fostering democratic institutions are crucial in creating a more stable and secure global environment.

Simultaneously, despite progress in civil rights, the quest for *social justice and the safeguarding of human rights* remain unresolved battles in many parts of the world including, surprisingly, "advanced" nations. Despite those advancements in civil rights, many individuals and groups still face discrimination and marginalization based on race, gender, ethnicity, sexual orientation and other identities. Ensuring social justice and human rights is an ongoing challenge, requiring vigilance and action from both governments and civil societies. This involves creating inclusive policies that protect the rights of all individuals, fostering diversity, and promoting equality. Education and dialogue are key tools in challenging stereotypes and prejudices, paving the way for more equitable societies.

As *technology advances* at an unprecedented pace, its potential to transform industries and societies is matched only by the *disruption* it brings to traditional ways of life as a global battle for domination ensues. Rapid technological advancement presents both opportunities and challenges. While it drives innovation and economic growth, it also disrupts traditional industries, leading to job displacement and social upheaval. The digital divide further exacerbates inequalities, as not all individuals and regions have equal access to technology and the skills needed to thrive in a digital world. Addressing these challenges requires strategic investments in education and training, as well as policies that safeguard data privacy and ensure fair competition

This is our world, a tapestry woven with threads of diversity and division. It's a place where breathtaking beauty and daunting challenges coexist, each influencing the other in ways that are often unexpected and profound. From bustling urban centers with towering skyscrapers to remote villages clinging to traditions, every corner of our planet presents a unique blend of cultures, ideas, and struggles. Yet, beneath the surface, we face common issues. Our societies are marked by growing divides, whether visible in the physical landscapes shaped by industrial pursuits or invisible like the social and economic barriers that separate us.

In this world, understanding fragmentation is key to bridging the gaps that keep us apart. What is fragmentation? Why do fragmented systems emerge, and what impacts do they have on our world? How is the larger societal fragmentation emerging in our day-to-day lives connected to my own scattered thoughts in this uncertain world, and my lack of clarity and focus?

As we journey in this book through these complexities, we might just discover not only the challenges but also the potential for connection and unity that lies just beyond the fragmented edges. Let us search together.

Chapter 2
Unraveling the Mosaic

Fragmentation. A seemingly simple term, yet it holds the weight of myriad worlds peeling away from their centers. At its essence, fragmentation refers to the process by which something whole is broken into parts, each piece a reflection of what once was unified. This concept, both intricate and ubiquitous, permeates every facet of our lives.

From the earliest dawn of civilization, fragmentation has played an undeniable role. Consider ancient empires that rose and crumbled, leaving behind a tapestry of cultures and languages—fragments of once expansive dominions. Yet these remnants give rise to new identities, cultures, and innovations, demonstrating how fragmentation, while dismantling, also creates fertile ground for development and diversity.

In our modern era, fragmentation is ever-present. This multifaceted phenomenon prompts us to rethink and reassess our interconnectedness. From the natural shifts beneath our feet to the intangible realms of our minds and societies, fragmentation touches every aspect of existence. While we have lightly explored some aspects of fragmentation in these introductory chapters, let's focus on providing a concise snapshot of primary areas, or domains, where fragmentation is evident. In the following snapshots, we explore the diverse landscapes where fragmentation unfolds, inviting us to understand its influences and implications. These glimpses into the physical, digital, societal, mental, and artistic domains set the stage for a deeper exploration, with a later chapter dedicate to each domain, into how each type of fragmentation within these domains shapes our realities and challenges us to seek unity in diversity.

Physical Fragmentation often manifests through geographical and environmental changes. Consider the natural phenomena of tectonic shifts, where Earth's plates move and fracture, creating new landscapes over geological time. These natural processes divide and redirect ecosystems, influencing biodiversity and climate patterns. In a later chapter we will explore the fragmentation of global mining. The man-made influence of urban sprawl serves as a key example of physical fragmentation induced by human activity. As cities expand into surrounding areas, they fragment natural habitats and agricultural lands, creating patchwork communities that challenge infrastructure and resource management. Types of physical fragmentation which are explored include: geological, ecological, urban, agricultural and geopolitical.

Holistic Human Fragmentation, experienced by many in an age of uncertainty and rapid change, emphasizes the internal struggles we face. In an age saturated with information, individuals experience cognitive overload, leading to fragmented attention and decision-making. The constant influx of data can cause stress and impair the ability to focus on meaningful tasks. Emotional fragmentation arises when individuals feel disconnected from themselves or others, influenced by social media and modern lifestyles. This disconnection affects mental health, relationships, and overall well-being. Types of holistic human fragmentation which are explored include: identity, emotional, cognitive, trauma-induced, relational, behavioral and health and safety.

Digital Fragmentation, a product of our technological age, is reshaping how we communicate and interact. The proliferation of digital platforms has led to a fragmented digital landscape. Social media, streaming services, and online communities often operate in silos, creating echo chambers where information and interactions are isolated within specific niches. This fragmentation disrupts traditional means of communication and interaction, leading to challenges in maintaining cohesive narratives and understanding in a rapidly developing digital environment. Types of digital fragmentation explored include: technological, regulatory, access, cultural/linguistic, platform, security and economic.

Narrative and Artistic Fragmentation is visible in the creative realms. In the art world, fragmentation is seen in the breaking of traditional forms and narratives. Movements like abstract art, postmodernism, and digital art explore fragmented expressions, challenging viewers to find meaning in dissonant or incomplete forms. Artistic fragmentation encourages experimentation and innovation, leading to new genres, styles, and mediums that reflect a complex, multifaceted world. Types of narrative/art fragmentation explored and exampled include: structural, temporal, thematic, visual, character and linguistic.

Societal Fragmentation emerges amidst political, economic, and cultural divides. Increasing polarization within societies is evident in social and political arenas, driven by factors like economic inequality, cultural identity, and political ideology. These divides fragment communities, influencing voting behaviors, social cohesion, and public policy priorities. More recent geopolitical events, such as Brexit and shifting alliances, exemplify societal fragmentation on a global scale. These shifts redefine relationships between nations, altering economic ties and cultural exchanges. Types of societal fragmentation explored include: economic, cultural, political, social, religious, informational and legal.

While we have provided above a few examples in each of these five domains, it is important to recognize the two levels of fragmentation: domains and types. Domains represent the broader arenas where fragmentation manifests, capturing the overarching themes and contexts—such as physical, digital, societal, mental/emotional, and narrative/art. These domains provide a structural framework that reflects the complex and diverse nature of fragmentation, allowing us to categorize and examine the phenomenon systematically.

Note that when discussing each domain above, we further identified specific types within that domain, which are the distinct manifestations or processes of fragmentation specific to each domain. Types delve into the particularities, illustrating the unique ways fragmentation occurs and affects entities within each domain. By organizing fragmentation into domains and their corresponding types, we can more effectively analyze and address the impacts across various contexts and scales, paving the way for nuanced insights and targeted interventions.

Domains of Fragmentation

Sample Lessons from Nature, Technology and Society

In biology, nature's resilient ecosystems exemplify how fragmentation can lead to interconnected networks. When a forest undergoes natural fragmentation due to events like fires or floods, it initially appears as destructive. However, this fragmentation often increases biodiversity, creating new habitats. Species migrate, adapt, and evolve, forming intricate food webs and cooperative relationships that foster ecosystem resilience. Over time, these interconnected ecosystems become more robust, as diversity leads to stability and adaptability.

In the digital realm, fragmentation has given rise to innovative technological ecosystems. Consider the open-source software movement: while proprietary software models exert centralized control, open-source projects like Linux harness the diverse contributions of fragmented global communities. This fragmentation fosters a collaborative spirit where independent developers contribute various pieces of code, collectively building robust, flexible software solutions. Such decentralized development systems exemplify how fragmentation leads to alignment around a shared vision, driving technological innovation.

Sociopolitical fragmentation, such as the dissolution of empires or federated states, often seeds cultural and national identity formation, bringing together a tapestry of cultures. For instance, the breakup of the Ottoman Empire led to the creation of modern nation-states across the Middle East and North Africa, each nurturing its own identity. While initial fragmentation spawned conflict, over time regional alliances and transnational organizations emerged, such as the Arab League, which aim to foster unity and cooperation among newly formed nations. This reflects a reimagined interconnectedness where independent entities align for collective security and prosperity.

In the realm of economics, fragmentation can create diverse networks of trade that drive globalization. As industries and markets evolved, economic fragmentation encouraged specialization. Countries and regions focused on areas of comparative advantage, leading to interconnected global supply chains. While each entity operates independently, the necessity of collaboration forms a cohesive global economy that relies on the alignment of fragmented economic units to function effectively.

These examples illustrate the inherent interconnectedness of fragmented systems, which will be more deeply addressed in the chapters focused on each domain, reminding us that while fragmentation may initially appear as disarray, it often sets the stage for new forms of unity and collaboration, encouraging adaptive strategies that spur innovation and resilience. This paradox of fragmentation—division leading to deeper, albeit more complex, unity—offers valuable insights for us to reflect upon.

In Summary ...

This brief introduction to the domains, and types within each domain, that are the focus of this book, set the stage for a deeper understanding of the role of fragmentation both historically and in the current world environment which is touching everyone.

As we embark on the steady unraveling of fragmentation across varied domains, it becomes evident that the essence of change is deeply entwined with this phenomenon. The very fabric of our world, in its fragmented form, suggests a powerful narrative of evolution—one where division and reassembly invoke a continuous cycle of adaptation.

The next chapter invites you to explore this dynamic interplay between fragmentation and change, delving into how the breaking apart of structures enables new pathways, shapes possibilities, and challenges us to perceive shifts as foundational to growth. Offering historical examples, this transition serves not as a conclusion, but as an invitation to explore and understand fragmentation as a quintessential component of change in its many forms.

Chapter 3
Fragmentation and Change

As we explore the dual nature of fragmentation, we further uncover its role as both a catalyst for destruction and a precursor to change. Let's engage Kurt Lewin's change model, such that we can better understand how fragmentation becomes an integral part of the cycle of adaptation and innovation. Embracing its complexities, we can navigate through the disorder it introduces, striving for a balance between disintegration and the potential for a more resilient reassembly.

While many change models have emerged through the years—several of which have been developed and implemented by the authors—we will use Kurt Lewin's simple model to explore the relationship of fragmentation and change. This model, a foundational framework for understanding organizational change, includes the stages of Unfreezing, Changing (or Transitioning), and Refreezing, providing a structured approach to managing change which can be highly relevant when addressing fragmentation and its impacts.

In the initial stage of unfreezing, the focus is on preparing individuals or organizations for change by acknowledging the need for transformation. If fragmentation is causing inefficiencies or reduced effectiveness, the unfreezing stage involves recognizing these problems and overcoming resistance to change. This includes building awareness about how fragmentation is detrimental and why change is necessary. For example, in a company experiencing digital fragmentation due to incompatible software systems, unfreezing would involve illustrating the costs of inefficiencies and rallying support for integrating a unified digital platform.

The Changing (or Transition) phase involves implementing the changes necessary to reduce fragmentation and improve efficiency and effectiveness. It requires transitioning from old patterns to new ones, and this process can include re-organizing physical systems, updating digital infrastructure, fostering societal cohesion, or promoting mental clarity. For societal fragmentation, this might include initiatives to build community networks or dialogue platforms that foster better understanding and collaboration across different societal groups.

The final state, Refreezing, is focused on solidifying new practices so that changes become part of the organization's culture or individual's routine, thus preventing fragmentation from reoccurring. This includes establishing new norms, procedures, or narratives that support the integrated system or cohesive community. In an artistic project, refreezing might involve establishing a coherent narrative framework or thematic guidelines to ensure future works avoid becoming fragmented, maintaining the integrity and impact of new art pieces.

Lewin's model emphasizes the continuous nature of change and the need to address underlying structures and attitudes, which is essential when dealing with fragmentation across various domains. By applying this change model, organizations and individuals can systematically tackle fragmentation, aligning resources and actions for improved outcomes.

While Lewin's model didn't come with specific instruction for intelligent use, applying it wisely requires certain considerations. First, context awareness, recognizing the unique aspects of the situation. Different organizations or scenarios may require tailored approaches to each stage of the model, taking into account cultural, structural, and human factors. [*Reference:* Burnes, B. (2004). Kurt Lewin and the Planned approach to Change: A Re-Appraisal. *Journal of Management Studies.* Burnes discusses the broader context in which Lewin's models can be applied and emphasizes the importance of understanding the organizational environment.]

Second, stakeholder engagement. Involving all relevant parties in the unfreezing stage can help ensure that the need for change is understood and that there is buy-in from those affected by the change. [*Reference:* Kotter, J. P. (1996). *Leading Change.* Boston, MA: Harvard Business Review Press. Kotter's book expands on the importance of creating a guiding coalition and engaging stakeholders during change processes.]

Third, communication. Throughout the change process, effective communication is key. Clearly articulating the reasons for change, the benefits, and the steps involved helps create synergy, building support and managing resistance. [*Reference:* Clampitt, P. G., DeKoch, R. J., & Cashman, T. (2000). A Strategy for Communicating About Uncertainty. *The Academy of Management Executive, 14*(4), 41-57. This paper focuses on the essential role of communication in managing change and uncertainty.]

Fourth, flexibility. While Lewin's model provides a structured approach, it's important to be flexible and adapt methods as needed in the changing stage. Being open to feedback and iterative adjustments can enhance the effectiveness of the change process. [*Reference:* Lewin, K. (1947). *Frontiers in Group Dynamics. Human Relations, 1*(1), 5–41. Lewin's foundational work on group dynamics explains the need for adaptability within change processes.]

Fifth, reinforcement, ensuring that new practices and behaviors are reinforced through policies, rewards, and cultural embedding to prevent reverting to old ways. This is the refreezing stage. [*Reference:* Schein, E. H. (2010). *Organizational Culture and Leadership*. San Francisco, CA: Jossey-Bass. Schein's work highlights how to effectively refreeze new behaviors and practices within an organization's culture.]

Overall, intelligent use of Lewin's model involves a thoughtful, context-sensitive application that considers the human elements of change—bringing those who the change affects into the strategy—and seeks to balance structure with adaptability.

At the same time Lewin's model was becoming popular, the idiomatic expression "don't throw the baby out with the bathwater" was catching attention, advising caution not to discard something valuable while disposing of something unwanted. It suggests that in the process of making necessary changes or discarding old, ineffective practices or items, one should be careful not to lose something worthwhile.

While the expression is often attributed to Abraham Lincoln—and it is possible that at some point he said it—the expression is believed to have originated from a German proverb, "das Kind mit dem Bade ausschütten," which in 1512 was used in a satire by Thomas Murner. The phrase was popularized in English primarily through translations and writings in the 19th century, capturing the idea in both literal and metaphorical contexts.

In the context of dealing with fragmentation and implementing change (such as through Lewin's Change Model), the phrase serves as a reminder to assess what aspects of the existing system, structure, or process are actually beneficial and worth preserving. While addressing issues of fragmentation—whether physical, digital, societal, or otherwise—it is crucial to ensure that valuable systems, practices, or relationships are not discarded in the pursuit of eliminating inefficiencies or improving effectiveness. This careful consideration helps maintain a balance, ensuring that valuable elements are integrated into new systems or practices.

In Historical Context

Historically, fragmentation has been as much a catalyst for change as it has been a force of disruption. To truly grasp the essence of fragmentation, we need to cast our gaze back through the annals of history, where the rhythm of breaking and mending has set the stage for the world we know today. From the crumbling relics of ancient empires to the scientific quests that spun whole elements into atoms, fragmentation is woven into the fabric of our collective past.

Think of the mighty Roman Empire, a colossus of governance, culture, and infrastructure. At its zenith, Rome was a mosaic of cultures, languages, and traditions. The *Pax Romana*, a period of relative peace, enabled the empire's exponential growth. However, as it expanded, internal fractures began to appear. Political corruption, economic instability, and overreliance on slave labor strained the empires fabric, sowing the seeds of its own fragmentation— stretching its resources, diversifying its populace, and eventually crumbling into a patchwork quilt of kingdoms and territories. This disintegration, however, was not an end; it was a transition. The fragments of Rome gave rise to new languages, customs, and nations, each inheriting a piece of that ancient civilization yet evolving into something distinct and new.

Similarly, the Han Dynasty in China experienced fragmentation after years of centralized power. Following internal strife, natural disasters, and economic struggles, the empire broke into the Three Kingdoms Period, characterized by constant warfare and cultural flourishing. This fragmentation stimulated advancements in technology, philosophy, and art—laying the groundwork for future reunification under later dynasties

The fragmentation theme persisted beyond ancient times, significantly impacting the formation of modern nation-states and political entities. For example, the Holy Roman Empire's gradual fragmentation due to religious conflicts, such as the Protestant Reformation, and political infighting among principalities, paved the way for the rise of modern European states. The Peace of Westphalia, which ended the Thirty Years' War, institutionalized the concept of national sovereignty, leading to a fragmented but more structured political map of Europe.

The exploration and subsequent colonization of new lands resulted in cultural fragmentation. European powers carved up continents, often disregarding existing social and ethnic compositions. This led to a fragmented world, with colonies adopting and adapting European ways while retaining their cultural identities, fostering a rich, albeit complex, creolized global culture.

The Industrial Revolution and the modern era have also been marked by significant fragmentation, manifesting through rapid technological, social, and geopolitical changes. For example, the fragmentation caused by the World Wars redrew borders and shifted global power balances. The breakup of empires post-World War I, such as the Austro-Hungarian and Ottoman empires, and the geopolitical shifts post-World War II, including the Cold War tensions, illustrate how conflict-driven fragmentation reshapes global dynamics.

In the 1980's the U.S. government was significantly influenced by a broader global trend toward efficiency and productivity enhancement, often referred to as "New Public Management" (NPM). This approach sought to apply private sector management techniques to public sector organizations, aiming to improve efficiency, effectiveness, and accountability in government operations.

Key characteristics and initiatives include deregulation, privatization, budget cuts and fiscal conservatism, management reforms, and technology and innovation. Under President Ronald Reagan's administration, there was a strong push for deregulation. The aim was to reduce the burden of government regulations on businesses, which was believed to stifle innovation and economic growth. Deregulation aimed to make both the economy and public sector more efficient by streamlining processes and reducing bureaucratic red tape. One of the coauthors has a piece of that "red tape" embedded in plastic that was awarded for her efforts in this movement.

As introduced above, the 1980s saw a trend toward privatizing certain government services. This was based on the belief that private companies could deliver services more efficiently than government agencies. Privatization initiatives included areas like waste management, transportation, and even some military functions. There was a strong emphasis on reducing government spending and cutting budgets to decrease the national deficit. This was partly driven by an ideology favoring smaller government and more efficient use of taxpayer money.

The government began adopting management practices from the private sector, including performance measurement and management by objectives. The idea was to foster a results-oriented culture within government agencies, focusing on outcomes and effectiveness. The adoption of new technologies was encouraged to improve efficiency within governmental operations. This aligned with the broader technological revolution taking place during this period, which saw the introduction and growing significance of computers and information systems.

On the positive side of the efficiency push, proponents have argued that these measures helped streamline government operations, reduced costs, and allowed for more innovation and responsiveness to public needs. On the negative side, critics of the efficiency drive have pointed out that certain essential services suffered from reduced funding and attention, potentially affecting service quality. Moreover the focus on efficiency sometimes led to trade-offs affecting effectiveness to include equity and access to public services. Let's explore that a bit deeper.

The Efficiency vs. Effectiveness Dilemma

The pursuit of efficiency within government operations in the U.S., particularly during the 1980s and continuing into subsequent decades, eventually highlighted several issues and limitations, prompting a reevaluation of efficiency-centric approaches. Here are some key discoveries and insights that emerged:

1. **Quality versus Efficiency**. An intense focus on efficiency led to a decline in the quality of services. By cutting costs and streamlining operations, some government functions suffered from reduced service levels, impacting citizens' satisfaction and trust in public institutions. An example is the Veterans Health Administration (VHA) scandal occurring in 2014. The VHA faced criticism for long wait times and inadequate care partly due to policies emphasizing efficiency and meeting performance metrics over patient care quality. *Reference:* Matthews, M. (2014, May 29). Why the VA's Imperfect Efficiency Fix Is My Favorite Newsweek Story of the Week. *Newsweek.*

   Fragmentation in service delivery systems, such as in healthcare or veteran services, can lead to a disconnect between different parts of the organization. This can result in a focus on efficiency metrics at the expense of service quality, as valuable information or processes become siloed and disjointed. In the VHA scandal, fragmented communication and processes likely contributed to diminished care quality, as parts of the system failed to work together cohesively.

2. **Unintended Consequences**. Efficiency drives, such as deregulation and privatization, occasionally resulted in unforeseen negative outcomes. For example, deregulating industries without sufficient oversight contributed to issues like environmental degradation or financial instability, evidenced by crises. For example, the Savings and Loan crisis of the late 1980s. Deregulation aimed at increasing financial sector efficiency inadvertently led to risky lending practices, contributing to the failure of numerous savings and loan institutions. *Reference:* Barth, J. R. (1991). *The Great Savings and Loan Debacle.* Washington, D.C.: American Enterprise Institute for Public Policy Research.

   Systemic fragmentation can obscure the broader implications of policy changes, leading to unintended consequences. When systems are not integrated, decision-makers might lack a comprehensive view of potential risks. The deregulation that contributed to the Savings and Loan Crisis reflects a fragmented approach to financial oversight, where individual policies did not account for their cumulative impact on the financial system.

3. **Equity Concerns**. Efforts to enhance efficiency often neglected considerations of equity and fairness. Policies that prioritized cost-saving measures sometimes disproportionately affected vulnerable populations, leading to increased inequality in access to essential services. An example is Welfare Reform under the Personal Responsibility and Work Opportunity Reconciliation Act (1996). Aimed at increasing efficiency by reducing government spending on welfare, this act raised concerns about reduced support for the poor and increased inequality. *Reference:* Weaver, K. (2000). Ending Welfare as We Know It. *Brookings Institution.*

Societal fragmentation can exacerbate inequities as different groups receive varying levels of attention and resources. Efficiency-driven reforms might overlook how fragmented access to resources adversely affects marginalized populations. Welfare reforms in the 1990s highlighted how fragmented policy implementation could deepen social divides, affecting different regions and communities unevenly.

4. **Loss of Public Sector Values.** The application of business-oriented principles to the public sector clashed with the primary mission of government agencies to serve the public good. This led to debates about the appropriateness of using private sector methods in public administration. An example is the privatization of prisons. The drive to run prisons more efficiently led to privatization, raising ethical concerns about profit motives overriding rehabilitative and humane treatment objectives. *Reference:* Selman, D., & Leighton, P. (2010). *Punishment for Sale: Private Prisons, Big Business, and the Incarceration Binge.* Lanham, MD: Rowman & Littlefield Publishers.

When privatization or efficiency measures lead to the fragmentation of values and objectives, the core public sector mission can be compromised. This division between profit goals and public service ethics can lead to ethical dilemmas. In privatized prisons, the fragmentation between economic and rehabilitative goals can result in neglect of public sector values focused on humane treatment and rehabilitation.

5. **Complexity of Public Problems.** Many public sector challenges are inherently complex and multifaceted, requiring solutions that prioritize effectiveness and adaptability over pure efficiency. This recognition led to the understanding that simplistic measures of efficiency could not

adequately capture the success of public policy. Consider the Hurricane Katrina Response in 2005. Emphasis on efficiency in emergency management led to inadequate preparation and response to Hurricane Katrina, illustrating the need for flexible and effective crisis management approaches. *Reference:* Dyson, M. E. (2006). *Come Hell or High Water: Hurricane Katrina and the Color of Disaster*. New York: Basic Books.

Fragmented emergency response systems can hinder effective management of complex public problems, as seen in natural disaster responses. Differences in agency communication and resource management can cause inefficiencies. The response to Hurricane Katrina illustrates how fragmentation among federal, state, and local agencies can delay or complicate effective crisis management.

6. **Sustainability.** Efficiency initiatives often prioritized short-term savings (with visibility) over long-term sustainability, leading to practices that were not environmentally or economically sustainable in the long run. The Flint Water Crisis of 2014 is an example. The decision to switch Flint's water supply to save money ignored long-term sustainability and public health impacts, leading to a major public health crisis and multiple and continuing deaths. *Reference:* Clark, A. (2016). How a Water Crisis in Flint, Michigan Became a Nationwide Scandal. *The Guardian.*

Fragmented decision-making can ignore long-term sustainability in favor of immediate efficiency gains. When departments or stakeholders are not aligned, holistic solutions that balance short-term efficiency with long-term viability may be overlooked. In the Flint water crisis, a fragmented approach to decision-making and oversight failed to address the long-term sustainability of water sourcing and infrastructure maintenance.

These realizations fostered a more balanced approach in public administration seeking to integrate efficiency with effectiveness, quality, and equity considerations. It also prompted a shift toward comprehensive assessments of public sector performance that included diverse metrics beyond just cost savings or output levels.

Ultimately, fragmentation proved a significant factor affecting both efficiency and effectiveness, particularly in contexts like business processes, technology systems, or even personal task management. It was discovered that fragmentation can lead to inefficiencies because it often involves a scattering of resources, efforts, or information. For example, in a business context, if different departments or teams are working in silos without proper communication or integration, it can result in duplicated efforts, wasted resources, or inconsistent data usage. This inefficiency can cost time and money and can slow down operations.

It was also discovered that fragmentation can hinder the ability to achieve desired outcomes. When processes or systems are fragmented, there may be gaps or overlaps that prevent the smooth completion of tasks. For example, in a fragmented customer service experience where information isn't shared across channels, customers might receive inconsistent information, leading to dissatisfaction and a failure to meet service goals.

By reducing fragmentation, you can significantly enhance both efficiency and effectiveness. You ensure resources are used optimally, and tasks are aligned with and contribute directly to your goals.

Have We Learned from the Past?

Unfortunately, memory appears short. The current actions by the U.S. government, involving random cuts and reorganization aimed at efficiency, exhibit similarities to past efforts seen in the 1980s and beyond. Here are a few parallels that highlight these similarities:

1. **Focus on Cost-Cutting.** The pursuit of fiscal efficiency often involves budget cuts or reallocations that might overlook the broader impact on service quality and accessibility. This can lead to similar quality-versus-efficiency dilemmas, where the drive for short-term savings can undermine long-term effectiveness.

2. **Unintended Consequences.** Similar to the unintended consequences seen in past initiatives, current budget cuts and reorganizations can lead to disruptions in essential services. These actions risk overlooking complex interdependencies within systems, leading to gaps or inefficiencies that may not be immediately apparent.

3. **Equity Issues.** Efforts focused purely on efficiency exacerbate inequalities, much like previous reforms that did not adequately consider the diverse needs of different population segments. When cuts are applied uniformly or without nuanced understanding, vulnerable groups might face disproportionate impacts.

4. **Loss of Mission Focus.** As in previous periods, there's a risk that overemphasizing efficiency in public sector management can lead to a divergence from foundational public service values. This can result in a fragmented focus where economic considerations overshadow the core mission of serving the public good.

5. **Fragmented Decision-Making.** Current reorganizations can suffer from the same fragmented approach that complicates effective governance seen in past crises like Hurricane Katrina. Without coordinated efforts and clear communication across different government levels, these changes might hinder rather than help efficiency.

6. **Sustainability Concerns.** Like in the Flint water crisis, efficiency-driven decisions today might prioritize short-term gains over long-term sustainability, potentially leading to unsustainable practices that could escalate costs or risks over time.

It's important for contemporary reforms to prioritize comprehensive evaluations that address both efficiency and the nuanced, multifaceted impacts of such changes. Integrated solutions that consider systemic interconnections and stakeholder needs can help avoid past pitfalls. The repetition of past strategies in government attempts to improve efficiency, despite encountering known pitfalls, appears to revolve around several complex factors.

First, **short-term focus**. There is often a strong emphasis on achieving immediate results, particularly in political cycles where stakeholders seek quick wins to demonstrate progress or fiscal responsibility. This can overshadow long-term strategic thinking that might better prevent repeated mistakes.

Second, **changing leadership and priorities**. Government leadership and priorities can change frequently with elections and policy shifts, leading to inconsistent application of lessons learned. New leaders may prioritize different aspects of governance, not always aligning with past insights.

Third, **structural challenges**. Overcoming entrenched bureaucratic processes and structural inertia can be difficult. Large systems often have complex interdependencies that resist change, making it challenging to sustainably implement lessons from past experiences.

Fourth, **economic and political pressures**. Economic downturns or shifts, as well as political agendas, can drive efficiency initiatives without a comprehensive evaluation of potential impacts. The pressure to reduce public spending or implement new reforms quickly can sideline deeper analysis.

Fifth, **knowledge transfer and institutional memory**. Organizations sometimes struggle with knowledge transfer and maintaining institutional memory, leading to a loss of valuable insights over time. Personnel turnover and lack of continuity in leadership can result in forgotten lessons. This is prevalent concurrent with the mass exodus underway in the U.S. government from reorganizations, resignations and firings.

Sixth, **overconfidence in new methods**. There can be an overreliance on new technologies or management approaches presumed to solve past problems, without fully understanding or addressing the reasons why previous efforts failed.

Seventh, **balancing complexity**. Addressing complex societal needs and systems is inherently challenging, and efforts to balance efficiency with other values such as equity and quality require nuanced approaches that can be difficult to execute.

Recognizing these pitfalls and fostering a culture of learning within government institutions can aid in developing more resilient and adaptive strategies that leverage past lessons effectively. In a democracy, government exists to serve the people, and unlike privately owned organizations that might prioritize efficiency or economic gain over purpose, public institutions must uphold their mission to benefit society first and foremost.

As we traverse the timeline of human history, we notice a recurring theme: fragmentation has been a process of deconstruction and reconstruction. It is through these cycles that societies, cultures, and individuals evolve, weaving new narratives from the threads of the old. Perhaps history offers us a roadmap, reminding us that the fragmented state of our world is neither unprecedented nor insurmountable. Instead, it is an opportunity to learn, adapt, and create anew.

With this promise of transformation, the chapters that follow will provide detailed examples of fragmentation underway in today's world, exploring the various types of fragmentation in the physical, holistic human, digital, narrative/art, and societal domains. We also explore the interplay among these fragmentations, recognizing that *fragmentation begets fragmentation*, as we slowly unravel how embracing fragmentation can lead to unexpected alignments, moving us toward yet-undiscovered futures.

Chapter 4
Physical Fragmentation

Delving deeper into the intricate tapestry of physical fragmentation, it becomes essential to explore the myriad ways in which our world is continuously shaped and reshaped. Fragmentation, whether by the subtle flow of natural processes or the more abrupt influence of human activity, manifests in diverse forms across geological, ecological, and sociopolitical landscapes.

Understanding the dual forces of natural and anthropogenic drivers in physical fragmentation is crucial for comprehensively assessing their impacts and managing their outcomes. Natural drivers, such as tectonic shifts and ecological dynamics, have historically shaped the planet's physical structures, evolving over millennia. However, in recent times, anthropogenic drivers like urbanization, industrialization, and geopolitical changes have accelerated and intensified these processes.

Natural Drivers	Anthropogenic Drivers	Interplay
Tectonic Activity	Urbanization	Tectonic movements can necessitate urban planning for seismic safety; urban development can also increase risk in tectonically active areas.
Volcanic Eruptions	Mining	Volcanic regions can contain valuable minerals, influencing mining activities; mining can disturb volcanic terrains and cause instability.
Erosion	Agriculture	Natural erosion shapes landscapes, while agricultural practices can both exacerbate and mitigate erosion.
Natural Disasters	Industrialization	Industrial areas may be prone to damage from natural disasters, prompting mitigation efforts; industrial activities can alter landscapes, affecting natural disaster dynamics.
Climate Changes	Geopolitical Changes	Shifts in climate impact geopolitical boundaries, as resource scarcity may drive political and economic fragmentation.

Recognizing the interplay between and among these forces allows for a holistic view: natural drivers may provide baselines and historical contexts, while human activities often amplify or alter these natural processes, creating unprecedented challenges. See the table above. By acknowledging both, policymakers, scientists, and communities can develop more nuanced strategies that address the root causes and cumulative effects of fragmentation, ultimately fostering sustainable development and conservation efforts.

With this understanding let's dig deeper into physical fragmentation, which can be categorized into various types, each with distinct characteristics and examples. Below, we explore a few common types, specifically, geological, ecological, urban, agricultural, geopolitical and industrial. Since each type has unique implications for the environment, biodiversity, and human societies, we also look at the relationship of each type to other domains of fragmentation as well as other types of physical fragmentation.

Geological Fragmentation

Geological fragmentation refers to natural processes. This includes phenomena like tectonic shifts, volcanic eruptions, and erosion, which naturally break, reshape, and fragment the Earth's crust over time. This includes the formation of mountain ranges and rift valleys due to tectonic activity.

An example is the East African Rift Valley which extends from the Afar Triangle in Ethiopia down to Mozambique in East Africa. This active continental rift zone is a prime example of geological fragmentation, where tectonic forces are splitting the African Plate into the Somali and Nubian Plates. [*Reference:* Chorowicz, J. (2005). The East African rift system. *Journal of African Earth Sciences, 43* (1-3), 379-410.]

As tectonic forces pull apart the Earth's crust, the formation of rift valleys creates new geological landscapes, resulting in deep valleys and elevated plateaus and accompanied by volcanic activity, leading to the formation of volcanoes such as Mount Kilimanjaro and Mount Kenya. The geography shifts influence human settlement patterns and offer agricultural opportunities while also posing risks, including earthquakes and volcanic eruptions, potentially threatening human life and infrastructure.

There are also significant cultural shifts, with the unique landscape and rich biodiversity of the East African Rift Valley attracting tourism, contributing to local economies. National parks in the area, like Serengeti and Ngorongoro Crater, are renowned for wildlife viewing and geological features. The landforms created by geological processes can hold cultural and spiritual significance for local communities, influencing their identities, traditions, and lifestyles.

Impact on Other Fragmentation Domains and Physical Types

- *Holistic Human:* The threat or occurrence of geological events can cause stress and anxiety for those living in affected areas.

- *Digital:* Geological fragmentation can disrupt digital infrastructure, such as internet cables and power lines, through natural events like earthquakes.
- *Art/Narrative:* Geological features often inspire artworks and narratives, symbolizing themes of change and endurance.
- *Societal:* It can reshape communities, forcing migrations, and altering historical settlement patterns.
- *Other Physical Types:* Further fragmentation can lead to soil erosion and land degradation, prompting secondary physical effects.

Ecological Fragmentation

Ecological fragmentation impacts ecosystems. This type of fragmentation involves the division of natural habitats into smaller, isolated patches—such as road construction dividing forests into smaller sections, often leading to loss of biodiversity and ecosystem functionality.

An example is the Brazilian Amazon in Northern Brazil. Deforestation due to agriculture, logging, and infrastructure development has led to significant fragmentation of the Amazon rainforest, impacting biodiversity and climate. Environmental and geological impacts include landscape formation, soil and hydrology changes, and volcanic activity. Biodiversity impacts include habitat diversification and speciation where populations of species are isolated, which can enhance biological diversity by creating new species over time.

Societal impacts offer agricultural opportunities and challenges, cultural and economic development, while simultaneously displacement and settlement patterns causing communities to relocate. Further, the fragmentation of the Earth's crust can lead to the formation of microclimates as different geological features create varying environmental conditions, influencing local weather patterns and biodiversity. [*Reference:* Laurance, W. F., et al. (2001). The future of the Brazilian Amazon. *Science, 291* (5503), 438-439.]

Impact on Other Fragmentation Domains and Physical Types

- *Holistic Human:* There is a sense of loss and anxiety concerning environmental degradation and its future impact.
- *Digital:* Loss of biodiversity can limit the inspiration drawn from nature for digital and technological innovations.
- *Art/Narrative:* Artists frequently depict ecological concerns, highlighting the fragility and importance of natural habitats.
- *Societal:* It disrupts ecosystems that communities depend on for resources, impacting livelihoods and cultures.

- *Other Physical Types:* Ecological fragmentation often leads to decreased resilience of ecosystems, exacerbating environmental challenges.

Urban Fragmentation

Urban fragmentation is human-induced change. Expansion of urban areas leads to the fragmentation of landscapes, creating isolated patches of natural habitats and altering land use. This can cause fragmented farmlands and provide challenging conditions for large-scale farming.

An example in the United States is the City of Los Angeles, California. Known for urban sprawl, the LA metropolitan area has expanded, fragmenting its surrounding natural habitats and agricultural lands. The sprawl of Los Angeles has led to the destruction of natural habitats, such as wetlands, grasslands, and coastal ecosystems. As urban areas expand, these ecosystems become fragmented, isolating wildlife populations and limiting their access to resources. Species such as the California gnatcatcher and various types of native plant life suffer from habitat degradation and increased edge effects (the transition area between two different ecosystems). Urban sprawl also contributes to a decline in local biodiversity. Fragmented habitats can limit gene flow between populations, leading to inbreeding and reduced resilience to environmental changes. The introduction of invasive species, often facilitated by human activity, can further threaten native species and ecosystems.

The expansion of impervious surfaces (like roads and buildings) has changed water drainage patterns, leading to increased runoff and flooding. This can create issues such as polluted stormwater runoff that affects local water bodies. Fragmentation of watersheds complicates natural water management and can harm aquatic ecosystems.

There are also significant social impacts. Urban fragmentation can lead to social isolation as neighborhoods become more disconnected from each other, resulting in a lack of community identity and diminished social cohesion. Residents may have limited access to natural green spaces, which are essential for mental health and community well-being. Fragmented urban areas often lead to increased reliance on cars, exacerbating traffic congestion and pollution. Long commutes contribute to air quality issues, which are exacerbated in a city like Los Angeles, known for its smog. Public transportation may be underdeveloped in fragmented regions, making it difficult for residents to access jobs, education, and services.

Further, Urban expansion can result in gentrification, displacing low-income communities as property values rise and land use changes. This can lead to socio-economic inequality and conflicts over land use, with vulnerable populations losing access to affordable housing and essential services as urban areas become more fragmented and commodified.

Economic impact is substantial. The fragmentation of agricultural lands surrounding Los Angeles makes it challenging for large-scale farming operations. Smaller, disconnected parcels may not provide the resources or infrastructure necessary for efficient agricultural production. This can impact food security in the region, as local agriculture becomes less viable due to urban encroachment.

Fragmentation may also affect tourism in the region. While urbanized areas like Los Angeles attract visitors, the loss of surrounding natural spaces diminishes attractions that rely on the region's environmental quality. Investment in urban infrastructure often focuses on development at the expense of parks and preserves, potentially reducing overall quality of life and tourism appeal.

More recently, large-scale fires have also changed the landscape, although the full ramification of this destruction and its effect on fragmentation will emerge with the rebuilding. [*Reference:* Fulton, W., et al. (2001). *Who's your city?: How the creative economy is making where to live the most important decision of your life*. Basic Books.]

Impact on Other Fragmentation Domains and Physical Types

- *Holistic Human:* Living in fragmented urban areas can lead to feelings of isolation or disconnect from communities.
- *Digital:* Can lead to unequal access to digital services across city regions, creating digital divides.
- *Art/Narrative:* Urban landscapes often feature prominently in modern art, reflecting themes of isolation and diversity.
- *Societal:* Promotes socio-economic disparities as different urban areas receive varying levels of investment and attention.
- *Other Physical Types:* Results in uneven development, contributing to further infrastructural fragmentation.

Agricultural Fragmentation

Agricultural fragmentation concerns land management and involves the breaking up of agricultural land into smaller plots, often due to inheritance, sale, or urban encroachment. As in urban fragmentation, fragmented farmlands provide challenging conditions for large-scale farming.

Let's use Punjab Province in Northern India as an example. Due to demographic pressures and land inheritance practices, the agricultural land in

Punjab has been fragmented into smaller and smaller plots. Positive impacts are increased smallholder participation, diverse crop cultivation, and localized farming practices. Small farms can adapt more quickly to local conditions and consumer preferences compared to larger farms, potentially improving food security at local levels.

Negative impacts include reduced economies of scale, increased inefficiency, soil degradation, access to technology and resources, and social inequality. Small plots often do not allow for economies of scale, and can lead to inefficiencies in farming practices, as smaller plots mean more time and energy spent on managing multiple fields, which reduces productivity and overall output. Continuous cultivation on smaller plots can lead to overexploitation of soil resource, resulting in soil degradation and diminished fertility over time. Additionally, smallholders may have limited access to modern farming technologies, quality seeds, and financial resources, which can hinder their capacity to improve yields and profitability.

Fragmentation of land can also exacerbate social and economic inequalities as those with more resources may be better positioned to succeed while smaller landholders struggle to make ends meet. [*Reference:* Sidhu, R. S., et al. (2005). Impact of land fragmentation on productivity in Punjab: Paradigm shifts in land use. *Indian Journal of Agricultural Economics, 60* (4), 509.]

Impact on Other Fragmentation Domains and Physical Types

- *Holistic Human:* Fragmentation may cause stress over agricultural viability and economic stability in rural communities.
- *Digital:* Small-scale farms may struggle to access the latest digital farming technologies, limiting agricultural innovations.
- *Art/Narrative:* Agricultural landscapes and the challenges faced by farmers are frequently depicted in literature and visual arts.
- *Societal:* Fragmentation can weaken traditional farming communities and practices, impacting food security.
- *Other Physical Types:* Contributes to inefficient land use, further fragmenting physical landscapes and ecological systems.

Geopolitical Fragmentation

Geopolitical fragmentation involves the creation of new borders. This type of fragmentation refers to the division of regions based on political conflicts, creating new national or administrative boundaries such as that which occurs in the breakup of countries, leading to newly defined states with distinct borders.

Such breakup occurred in Yugoslavia, located in the Balkan Peninsula in Southeast Europe. The disintegration of Yugoslavia in the 1990s resulted in the eventual creation of new countries, altering geopolitical boundaries and leading to new international borders. Slovenia declared independence in June 1991, followed by a brief conflict known as the Ten-Day War. Independence for Croatia, also declared in June 1991, sparked significant violence, particularly during the Croatian War of Independence. Bosnia and Herzegovina, another republic, declared independence in March 1992, resulting in a brutal conflict known as the Bosnian War that involved multiple ethnic groups and extensive ethnic cleansing.

North Montenegro, previously known as Macedonia, was one of the constituent republics of Yugoslavia. It declared independence in September 1991, but did so with less violence compared to others, largely achieving independence without significant conflict. Montenegro, also a republic within Yugoslavia, initially remained part of the union with Serbia after the breakup of the Federal Republic of Yugoslavia (later the State Union of Serbia and Montenegro) until it declared independence in June 2006. Serbia, one of the largest and most influential republics in Yugoslavia, became the principal successor state to the Federal Republic of Yugoslavia, alongside Montenegro. Serbia retained its status and continues to exist as an independent nation today.

Impact on Other Fragmentation Domains and Physical Types

- *Holistic Human:* Geopolitical changes can sow uncertainty and anxiety within populations.
- *Digital:* Creates barriers to digital communication and collaboration across new or changing borders, affecting internet governance and connectivity.
- *Art/Narrative:* Often the subject of powerful narratives and art, detailing stories of division and unity.
- *Societal:* Leads to political and ethnic tensions, affecting national identities and social cohesion.
- *Other Physical Types:* Changing borders can lead to physical separation of communities, affecting ecosystems and regional planning.

Industrial Fragmentation

Industrial fragmentation includes resource extraction. This refers to human activities, like both large and small scale mining and logging, that fragment landscapes and ecosystems to access natural resources. An example is the mountaintop removal (MTR) mining in Appalachia in the Eastern United

States. This form of coal mining fragments the Appalachian Mountains' natural landscapes, exemplifying the substantial ecological and social impacts of industrial fragmentation. The ecological impacts are vast. Let's use this example to explore these impacts in greater detail. They include:

(1) *Habitat Destruction.* MTR involves the complete removal of mountaintops to access coal deposits, leading to the destruction of diverse ecosystems. Forests and habitats for wildlife are obliterated, resulting in the loss of flora and fauna that rely on these ecosystems

(2) *Los of Biodiversity.* The destruction of habitats contributes to a decline in biodiversity. Species that are endemic to the Appalachians or have limited ranges are particularly vulnerable to extinction due to habitat loss and fragmentation.

(3) *Soil Erosion.* The removal of vegetation and the alteration of the landscape increase soil erosion. This can lead to sediment runoff into local waterways, affecting water quality and the health of aquatic ecosystems.

(4) *Water Pollution.* The mining process generates toxic waste, which can leach into nearby streams and rivers. Heavy metals and other pollutants from mining sites contaminate water sources, affecting aquatic life and posing risks to human health.

(5) *Altered Water Flow.* The removal of mountaintops and changes to the topography can disrupt natural water flow patterns, leading to altered hydrology. This can exacerbate flooding and reduce the availability of clean water in surrounding areas.

(6) *Air Pollution.* Dust and emissions from machinery and transportation associated with mining operations can contaminate the air, contributing to respiratory problems and other health issues in local communities.

The social impacts are equally egregious. For example:

(1) *Community Displacement.* MTR often requires the relocation of communities, uprooting families and disrupting long-standing social networks. The cultural and historical ties to the land are severed, leading to a sense of loss and identity crisis.

(2) *Health Issues.* Communities surrounding MTR sites face significant health risks due to air and water pollution. Increased rates of respiratory illnesses, cardiovascular diseases, and other health problems have been reported in areas affected by MTR.

(3) *Economic Impacts.* While MTR may provide short-term economic benefits through job creation, the long-term consequences can be detrimental. The depletion of natural resources can lead to economic

instability, and the loss of biodiversity can affect tourism and other sustainable industries.

(4) *Social Inequality.* The benefits of coal mining often accrue to corporations and external stakeholders, while local communities bear the brunt of the environmental and social costs. This can deepen social inequality and create conflicts over resource management and environmental justice.

(5) *Activism and Resistance.* The adverse effects of MTR have led to increased activism and resistance among local communities and environmental organizations. Community coalitions have formed to advocate for sustainable practices and the protection of local ecosystems.

(6) The destruction of *cultural landscapes and values* associated with the land can lead to a diminished sense of place and belonging. Traditional practices, heritage, and cultural identities linked to the landscape may be threatened or lost.

Mountain Top Removal Mining: Uglifying Nature

As can be seen, while MTR may provide economic benefits, the long-term consequences result in significant ecological degradation and profound social challenges, underscoring the need for more sustainable resource extraction practices and policies that prioritize the well-being of both the environment and the communities affected.

Impact on Other Fragmentation Domains and Physical Types

- *Holistic Human:* Impacts communities through job losses or environmental harm, leading to mental health challenges.
- *Digital:* May drive digital innovation as industries seek more efficient and less invasive resource extraction methods.
- *Art/Narrative:* Inspires art and narratives critiquing industrial practices and their impact on nature and society.
- *Societal:* Can cause socio-economic disparities between resource-rich areas and those affected by environmental degradation.
- *Other Physical Types:* Intensifies physical fragmentation through land degradation, pollution, and habitat destruction.

In Summary,

Understanding these various types of fragmentation allows us to appreciate how interconnected systems react and adapt to both gradual and sudden changes, setting the stage for the profound examples and implications that follow.

In synthesizing these connections, we can see that the physical fragmentation of landscapes not only reshapes the environment but also deeply influences other facets of human experience and society. This interconnectedness must be considered in policy-making and community planning to address the broader implications of fragmentation across all areas.

Chapter 5
Hidden Layers:
Tales from the Mines

We are going to use mine fragmentation to further explore the interconnectedness of the domains of fragmentation. In examining the extensive reach of mining, particularly within economically challenged regions, the multifaceted impacts on physical and holistic human fragmentation become starkly apparent. Mining operations in these areas often act as catalysts for even deeper levels of fragmentation, intertwining with and exacerbating existing social, economic, and environmental divisions.

The extraction of valuable minerals and resources, while potentially boosting local economies, frequently comes at significant costs. These can include the disruption of natural landscapes, questions of land ownership, and the division of communities. As we delve into specific mining examples, we must consider how these activities not only fracture the Earth's surface but also contribute to broader patterns of fragmentation that ripple throughout various aspects of society.

We offer five examples below of different aspects of mining around the world. Each example provides a story representing a workday in that particular mine. While it is certainly not necessary to read all five, we wanted to provide you the opportunity to recognize the reoccurring patterns of fragmentation and the impact economic gain has on holistic human health and safety, a focus in the following chapter. We begin with cobalt and copper mining.

Cobalt and Copper Mining in the DRC

The Democratic Republic of Congo (DRC) is one of the richest countries in terms of natural resources, yet it remains economically poor. The region around Katanga is famous for its cobalt and copper mines. Many laborers work in artisanal and small-scale mining (ASM), which often involves rudimentary methods and manual labor. Working conditions can be hazardous with minimal safety measures, and child labor has been reported. What might a workday look like?

A Day in the Mines of Katanga, DRC

In the heart of the Democratic Republic of Congo, deep within the Katanga region, lies the sprawling open mines of Kolwezi. The sun rises early, casting long shadows that mark the start of yet another laborious day for the miners in the copper and cobalt fields. Among the workforces is a man named Daniel, who begins his day at dawn, seven days a week, under the glaring African sun.

Each morning, Daniel makes his way to the mine along with dozens of others, some traveling on foot for miles. The air buzzes with conversations in various local dialects, mixing anticipation and the slight dread of the hard work ahead. Daniel shoulders his gear—a simple pickaxe, a shovel, and a few worn-out sacks, tools that are basic yet essential for the job.

Kolwezi's landscape is marred by deep, open pits, carved meticulously over years by miners like Daniel. Without the sophisticated machinery found in wealthier nations, the process is painstakingly manual. Each miner finds a spot, a small patch within the vastness of the mine, and begins the task of extracting the precious ore. They break the rock face with handheld tools, each swing shaking loose fragments of copper and cobalt

As the day progresses, a palpable fatigue sets in. The heat is relentless, with temperatures often soaring above 30 degrees Celsius. Water is scarce, and breaks are infrequent. Daniel and his fellow laborers pause for brief moments to drink from shared bottles, their hands dusty, faces streaked with sweat and grime.

The real challenge lies beneath the surface, where the minerals are concealed within rocky veins, fragmented amidst less coveted rock. Daniel's trained eyes spot these, hacking away the unwanted rocks to reveal glittering seams of copper and cobalt. The fragmentation is both literal and symbolic—valuable elements interspersed amongst the useless—which mirrors the challenging life of the miners, filled with scattered moments of respite and hardship.

Yet beyond the physical labor, the mines of Kolwezi tell a story of broader socioeconomic fragmentation. Many issues emerge: the stark disparity between the riches of the land and the poverty of its people, the lack of safety measures resulting in frequent accidents, and the persistent undercurrent of exploitation in artisanal mines. Child labor is not uncommon, with young boys working alongside men, learning quickly but at great personal cost.

As the afternoon wears on, Daniel and his fellow laborers sort through their day's collection. They separate the valuable fragments, placing each piece of extracted cobalt and copper into sacks. The sacks weigh heavily, not just from the sheer physical burden but also the weight of familial dependency they represent. Each haul is a day's wages, a tenuous financial lifeline.

By evening, the sacks are collected and hauled away by middlemen who transport them to larger processing facilities. Returning home as the sun sets, Daniel reflects on another day in Kolwezi. For Daniel and his family, the cobalt and copper are more than mere minerals; they are hopes for education, ambitions for better healthcare, and dreams of futures unburdened by poverty and exploitation.

This story of Kolwezi is but one narrative among many within the DRC, where the hands of miners painstakingly extract hope from the earth's fragmented bounty, bridging the divide between a land rich in resources and a population seeking prosperity.

Now, leaving Daniel and his family, where does the cobalt and copper go and how is it used?

Journey and Processing

The raw ore that miners like Daniel extract is first transported to local processing facilities. Here, the ore undergoes smelting and refining to separate the metals from impurities. This often involves crushing the ore and subjecting it to chemical processes that concentrate the metals. Once refined, the metals are often exported.

The DRC serves as a key supplier of cobalt and copper to international markets. Major importing countries include China, which is among the largest consumers and processors of these metals. The metals might undergo further refinement and are converted into forms usable by various industries. Cobalt is often processed into cobalt sulfate or oxides, and copper into sheets, wires, or rods, ready for manufacturing.

One of the most significant uses of cobalt is in the production of rechargeable lithium-ion batteries. These are critical components in smartphones, laptops, and electric vehicles (EVs), supporting the global shift towards renewable energy solutions. Cobalt is also used in creating superalloys for jet engines and gas turbines, due to its ability to withstand high temperatures.

Copper's excellent electrical conductivity makes it indispensable in the electrical industry, used in wiring and motors. It's also used for plumbing, roofing, and as part of the anti-corrosion layers in marine environments. Copper is essential in the electronics industry and has increasing applications in electric vehicles and renewable energy systems such as wind turbines and solar panels.

The demand for cobalt and copper highlights the importance of sustainability in mining and recycling. Many industries are focusing on reducing dependency on freshly mined materials by improving recycling methods for batteries and electronics. For the DRC, the export of these minerals is a vital source of economic income. However, ensuring that this wealth translates into broader economic development and improved living conditions for mining communities remains a critical challenge.

The journey from the mines to diverse industries around the world illustrates not only the essential role these materials play in modern life but also underscores the global interconnectedness of resources and technology.

Mika Mining in India

India is a major producer of mica, a mineral used in electronics, cosmetics, and paints. Key mining areas include the states of Jharkhand and Bihar. In these regions, informal mining operations often employ local villagers under tough conditions. The work is labor-intensive, and illegal operations can mean lack of proper oversight and potential exploitation.

A Day in the Mica Mines of Jharkhand, India

In the remote hills of Jharkhand, India, the morning sun peeks through dense forests, casting dappled light onto the dirt paths winding toward the mica mines. Here, in the heart of India's mica belt, the day begins early for miners like Sita, a determined woman who shoulders the responsibility of supporting her family.

As dawn breaks, Sita gathers her tools—a homemade pick and a few tattered sacks—and begins her trek to the mines, joined by neighbors and friends from her village. The path is steep and uneven, carved out by countless footsteps over many years. Children, their faces gleaming with anticipation or trepidation, walk alongside their parents, sharing both conversation and the burden of working to support their families.

Reaching the mica-rich hills of Giridih, the landscape reveals shallow pits and small caves, some reinforced precariously with timber and stones. These makeshift mines are often operated informally and without regulation, posing safety risks to the laborers. Sita selects a familiar spot and begins her day's work, her hands sifting through the earth in search of mica flakes.

The work is meticulous. Mica is found in thin, layered sheets embedded in the rocky terrain, requiring careful extraction to minimize breakage. This fragmentation lies at the heart of the task—separating the glossy sheets of mica from the rough, worthless stone. Each delicate layer adds to the value of the haul, destined for a variety of industries worldwide.

Conditions are rugged. The thin shafts often lack proper ventilation, and the risk of cave-ins looms large. With little access to protective gear, cuts and bruises are a common part of mining life, accepted with stoic resilience by Sita and her peers.

The midday sun is relentless, and the miners pause briefly to rest and share modest meals—usually simple chapatis and lentils. These breaks offer a time to exchange news, share aspirations, and momentarily forget the weight of their tasks. Yet, alongside physical exhaustion, the miners face broader issues: exploitation by local traders, inconsistent income, and the ever-present specter of illegal child labor, which NGOs and government initiatives strive to combat.

As the day lengthens, Sita continues her meticulous work, her fingers deftly separating the valuable mineral from the earth. The mica sheets shimmer in the sunlight, their reflective surfaces glinting with the promise of economic survival. By evening, the collected mica is gathered, carefully bundled into sacks. These are sold to local agents who transport them to larger processing centers. Mica from Jharkhand travels far, feeding into global supply chains

Returning home at dusk, Sita reflects on the demands and rewards of her work. The mica she helps unearth plays a small but vital role in an array of products, bridging the gap between her rural life and the broader world. Yet, she hopes for a future where the wealth of her region translates into better living conditions, education, and health care, ensuring that the hard work put into mining mica becomes a foundation for community development rather than just survival.

Journey and Processing

After miners like Sita collect the mica, it is typically sold to local agents who gather raw mica from various small-scale operations. This collected mica undergoes an initial sorting process where workers manually separate the sheets based on size, quality, and color. The sorted mica is then transported to larger processing centers, often located in nearby cities. From here, it is exported globally to countries with significant manufacturing industries such as the United States, Germany, and Japan. India remains one of the largest exporters of sheet mica in the world. At processing facilities, the mica is cleaned and further refined. It is cut and split into standardized sizes according to the needs of various industries. This refined mica is then packaged and shipped to different manufacturing sectors.

Mica's sparkling and reflective properties make it highly desirable in cosmetics. It is used as a pigment extender for achieving shimmer in products such as eyeshadows, blushes, and highlighters. Its fine texture and natural sheen add a luxurious appeal to personal care products.

Mica's excellent dielectric strength and thermal stability make it perfect for use in electronic equipment. It is used in insulators and as a filler in circuit boards and capacitors, helping devices function safely by managing heat and electrical charges. And due to its durability and resistance to moisture, mica is used in paints and coatings to provide a glossy finish. It's also incorporated into automotive paints and used as a reinforcing agent in building materials, contributing to the manufacturing of lightweight, strong, and weather-resistant composites.

The demand for ethically sourced mica highlights the need for greater transparency in the supply chain. Efforts are underway by nonprofits and multinational companies to ensure fair labor practices and to reduce environmental impact through improved mining practices. While mica mining provides essential income for thousands of families, the challenge remains to ensure that these communities see sustainable economic development. Educational programs and improved health services are crucial initiatives funded by efforts directed at using mica revenue for broader community gain.

The journey from extraction to end-use products highlights the intricate and far-reaching impact of mica. This essential mineral finds its way from the hands of miners like Sita, through complex global supply chains, into everyday products, linking their lives to consumers around the world in an endless cycle of production and consumption.

Coltan (Tantalum) in Rwanda

Coltan is a key component in electronic devices, and the region is a significant global supplier. Mining operations are often small-scale and manual, with miners working in potentially unsafe environments. There have been international concerns regarding the financing of conflicts through mining profits.

A Day in the Coltan Mines of Rwanda

In the mist-covered hills of Rwanda lies a region rich in natural resources, where the dense forests conceal the valuable mineral known as coltan. This mineral, pivotal for modern electronics, is at the heart of a grueling industry. Among the workers in this setting is Emmanuel, a miner whose daily life reflects the hardships and hopes tied to this trade.

At dawn, the air is thick with humidity as Emmanuel sets out from his village nestled outside the town of Nyaragusu. His journey to the mine is a trek through uneven forest paths, accompanied by fellow miners who tread the path somberly, knowing the demands of the day ahead. The rhythmic chirping of forest birds is a stark contrast to the laborious task that awaits them.

Upon reaching the mines, Emmanuel dons his simple gear—a headlamp, worn-out boots, and a makeshift pick. The mining area is an informal artisanal operation, a patch of cleared forest ground dotted with holes of varying depths. These shallow pits, created by hand, reveal the earth's bounty of coltan, but not without a price.

Tales from the Mines

Emmanuel begins his day by digging through the clay-rich soil with his pickaxe, working alongside men and sometimes women and children who help sift and separate the dense coltan ore from the surrounding earth. Fragmentation dominates this process, both in the literal sense—coltan particles extracted from soil—and the symbolic, as individuals are pieced within a fragmented economy.

Each swing of the pickaxe is labor-intensive, driven by the need to break through layers of earth. With no mechanical help, this is back-breaking work, demanding physical stamina and focus. Emmanuel's muscles strain against the consistent pressure, sweat darkening his shirt despite the coolness of the shaded forest.

As the sun arcs high above the forest canopy, the heat and exhaustion intensify. A meager lunch break provides temporary respite, often comprising rice or cassava shared communally among the miners. Here, camaraderie blooms amidst adversity; laughter, stories, and sometimes songs fill moments of rest.

Yet the challenges are many: the risk of pit collapses is ever-present due to the lack of structural support, unprotected under a precarious ceiling of earthen material. Potential dangers abound with exposure to dust leading to respiratory issues, and long hours without sufficient safety measures add to the toll on Emmanuel's and his colleagues' health.

Despite fatigue and the inherent dangers, the work continues. Emmanuel methodically separates the coltan particles from the dross, a meticulous task that demands sharp eyes and patient hands. The mineral's surprisingly metallic gleam against the dark soil signifies hope—its market value a critical source of income for families dependent on this trade.

By sunset, the day's collection of coltan is gathered into sacks, weighed against a scale that measures daily output in economic terms. These are sold to local traders, initiating coltan's journey from the mines to the global marketplace.

Reflecting on a day's work, Emmanuel and his fellow miners embody both resilience and vulnerability in their toil. The coltan extracted from Rwanda's earth represents both the physical cost paid by individuals and the invisible links creating the digital world's infrastructure—a reminder of the human stories embedded within each electronic device's components.

Journey and Process

The collected coltan is transported to regional centers where it undergoes initial cleaning and concentration. This refined material is then exported to major processing hubs, primarily in Asia and North America. Coltan is processed into tantalum powder, a key component for manufacturing capacitors within electronics. Its high capacitance and reliability make it indispensable for smartphones, computers, and other digital devices. Tantalum's corrosion-resistant properties extend its use into aerospace components and automotive electronics, underscoring its versatility and importance.

There is a growing movement toward ensuring coltan extraction adheres to sustainable and ethical practices, including initiatives to trace sourcing and ensure fair compensation for laborers. However, coltan mining, while financially pivotal for individual miners and communities, presents enduring challenges regarding equitable distribution of wealth and improvement of living standards.

Gemstone Mining in Madagascar

Madagascar is known for its variety of gemstones, including sapphires and rubies. Mining is predominantly artisanal, involving manual digging and sifting. Many miners operate without proper equipment, making the work both laborious and dangerous.

A Day in the Gemstone Mines of Madagascar

In the remote regions of Madagascar, where verdant forests meet rocky outcrops, lies the epicenter of a vibrant yet perilous industry—gemstone mining. Here, under a sky that shifts from blue to overcast unpredictably, miners like Rakoto embark on daily expeditions into the heart of the earth to uncover hidden treasures. The town of Ilakaka, a once quiet village, has transformed into a bustling mining hub.

Morning in Ilakaka begins with the sounds of roosters crowing and the steady murmur of the Andranovory River. As sunlight pierces through the fragile canopy of trees, the streets come alive with miners readying themselves for the day's grueling work, their faces etched with both hope and resignation.

For Rakoto, a veteran of the mines, the morning routine is one of practiced efficiency. He checks his gear—a well-worn pickaxe and a handwoven basket for sifting dirt—and kisses his young daughter on the forehead before setting off. Despite the challenges, this journey into the depths of the earth is as much a bid for survival as it is for prosperity.

As Rakoto joins a throng of fellow miners, their conversations echo in a blend of Malagasy and French, discussing rumors of new deposits and the ever-changing market prices of sapphires. The path to the mines involves trekking through dense forests and crossing makeshift bridges. Each step is a reminder of the risks; bandits have been known to prey on the miners, and accidents due to inadequate operational safety measures are all too common.

Once at the site, the real test begins. The act of mining—digging into the hard earth, sometimes overturning tons of rock with nothing but a spade and raw determination—is a physical and mental ordeal. The ground is unforgiving; it conceals its treasures stubbornly, and any false move can lead to a collapse.

A single shift in the earth can trap the miners, a constant shadow over their every action. The heat inside the pits is suffocating, and the absence of proper ventilation aids little in alleviating their ordeal.

Hours pass amidst sweat and dust. The sun reaches its zenith, casting long shadows across the rugged terrain. Rakoto pauses briefly to drink water and eat a small loaf of bread, staring out over the landscape that both sustains and threatens him. This momentary reprieve is not just for his body but his spirit— a renewal of his resolve.

By late afternoon, the yield of the day is assessed. Rakoto's finds vary from day to day; today, a few small sapphires glimmer in his hand, promising a week of food and perhaps a small celebration. Yet, he knows others may not be so fortunate. Bright stones gleaned from the earth symbolize not just wealth but also the caprice of fate.

As dusk approaches and the miners begin their trek back to Ilakaka, the air cools and fills with the scent of evening fires. Laughter and chatter intermingle, a defiant narrative woven against the day's hardships. Each miner carries with him not just gems, but shared stories of perseverance and dreams carved from the very rock they toil.

For Rakoto, the return home means another night with his family, another day survived in the challenging yet captivating world of Madagascar gem mining—a place where beauty and danger dance hand in hand, revealing the depths of human resilience against the backdrop of a land fiercely beautiful and truly untamed.

Journey and Process

After being mined, the rough gemstones are brought to local markets, often in Ilakaka, for initial sorting and valuation. They are examined for quality attributes such as color, clarity, and size, influencing their market value. Once sold to traders, the stones are exported to international gem markets, where they undergo precise cutting and polishing. Major refining hubs include cities in Thailand, Sri Lanka, and Belgium, where advanced techniques transform rough stones into dazzling gemstones.

The primary application for these gemstones is in fine jewelry. Sapphires and rubies, for instance, become the centerpiece of engagement rings, necklaces, and earrings, adding significant value and beauty. Beyond adornment, gemstones can also be used in various technological applications, including infrared optics, due to their unique physical properties.

Similar to coltan, there is increasing advocacy for responsible mining practices in the gemstone industry. Efforts are underway to implement fair trade certifications that ensure gemstones are ethically sourced, with transparent supply chains benefiting both local communities and environmental conservation. While gemstone mining offers a vital source of income for many in Madagascar, significant challenges remain in achieving equitable wealth distribution. The sector often suffers from imbalances where intermediaries reap substantial profits compared to the miners themselves. Enhancing miners' economic conditions is crucial, alongside stimulating local economies through infrastructure development supported by mining revenues.

And one more example. How could we leave out gold mining?

Gold Mining in Burkina Faso

Burkina Faso has grown as a gold producer, with the precious metal bringing significant revenue. Artisanal gold mining is common, with workers often exposed to hazardous substances like mercury, used in the gold extraction process. Children and women are also sometimes involved in mining activities.

A Day in the Gold Mines of Burkina Fasco

As the first light of dawn illuminates the vast savannah of Burkina Faso, the rhythmic sound of pickaxes against rock echoes through the air. In this land of golden promise, countless families depend on the riches hidden deep within the earth to sustain their lives. The scenario unfolds in a small mining community near the village of Kouékouesso, where the line between hope and hardship is finely drawn.

In this village, the men, women, and even children rise early, gathering their rudimentary tools—shovels, buckets, and pans—and set off toward the panning sites that dot the landscape. Among them is Amadou, a young father, his wife Awa, and their daughter Fati. The family, like many others, is entangled in the relentless pursuit of gold, a pursuit fraught with danger and health risks.

The artisanal mining operation is a stark contrast to the mechanized processes seen elsewhere. Miners tunnel into the earth, creating labyrinthine shafts, and sift through the unearthed soil looking for valuable ore. The day's labor begins with removing vast quantities of earth by hand, an arduous task that leaves little room for error or pause.

Once the ore is collected, it is time to extract the gold. This is where the real risks emerge. Mercury, a toxic substance, plays a central role in the extraction process. Amadou carefully mixes mercury with the crushed ore, watching as it forms an amalgam with the gold particles—a rudimentary process passed down through generations. As heat is applied to separate the gold, mercury vapors rise invisibly, posing a grave threat to anyone nearby.

Awa supervises the amalgamation, her hands stained from years of handling mercury. She knows the risks but economic necessity leaves her with little choice. Like many women in the community, her involvement is crucial, yet it exposes her to the same health hazards faced by her male counterpart.

Young Fati, though keen to learn her letters and numbers at school, often finds herself alongside her parents, tasked with simple chores like panning tailings. For children, the exposure to such environments is perilous; their developing bodies are particularly vulnerable to the adverse effects of mercury and other harsh conditions.

As the sun traverses the sky, the family's efforts yield some small nuggets, shining with promise yet laden with the weight of sacrifice. By sunset, they make their way back home, their strides tired but tinged with a glimmer of hope for a better tomorrow.

While gold brings much-needed revenue to Burkina Faso, supporting local economies and livelihoods, stories like that of Amadou's family highlight the complexities inherent in this industry. The delicate balance between economic survival and health underscores the urgent need for safer mining practices and processes to protect the most vulnerable, ensuring that progress in Burkina Faso does not come at the cost of its people's well-being.

Journey and Process

Once extracted, the artisanal gold is often sold to local collectors or traders who visit the mining sites. It is then transported to regional centers where it undergoes preliminary assessments and is sold in bulk. From the regional centers, the gold is moved to official refineries, often located in larger cities. Here, it is refined to increase purity, ridding the gold of impurities and preparing it for international markets. These refineries can be located domestically or in foreign processing hubs, offering advanced techniques to achieve high-grade purification.

A significant portion of refined gold is crafted into jewelry and luxury pieces. Gold's aesthetic appeal and status as a symbol of wealth and prestige make it a favored choice for rings, necklaces, and other adornments. Beyond aesthetics, gold's excellent conductivity and resistance to corrosion make it highly valuable in the electronics sector. It is used in making connectors, switches, and other components in devices ranging from smartphones to aerospace technologies. Gold is also crucial in financial markets as a store of value. It is minted into coins and bars, traded globally as an investment asset, and used by central banks to diversify reserves.

There is an expanding focus on ensuring that gold mining operations adhere to ethical and sustainable practices. This includes initiatives to reduce environmental degradation and improve safety and health conditions for miners, minimizing the use of harmful substances like mercury. While gold mining contributes significantly to Burkina Faso's revenue, the equitable distribution of this wealth remains a critical issue. Efforts are being made to ensure that the benefits impact local communities positively through job creation, infrastructure development, and improvements in social services. Equally important is addressing the issue of child labor and ensuring safe work environments for women and other vulnerable populations involved in the mining process.

Fragmentation Begets Fragmentation

Fragmentation in one area leads to fragmentation in other areas, often creating a cycle of compounding issues. In the context of mines in poorer countries, physical fragmentation, such as broken or divided physical spaces and infrastructure, often goes hand-in-hand with social, economic, and political fragmentation.

For example, the physical fragmentation of land due to mining can lead to social fragmentation, as communities are displaced or divided. This can exacerbate economic disparities, creating further inequality and limiting access to resources and opportunities. Economic fragmentation can lead to political fragmentation, where governance is weak, laws are poorly enforced, and corruption may be rampant. This environment can further perpetuate issues like child labor and unsafe working conditions.

Moreover, each form of fragmentation reinforces the others. Poor governance can stall economic development, which might prevent the construction of safe infrastructure, perpetuating physical fragmentation. Similarly, when communities are socially fragmented, it can be challenging to build a unified response to advocate for better conditions. Thus, it becomes a cycle where each type of fragmentation feeds back into itself or influences another type, making it challenging to resolve without addressing all facets simultaneously.

Looking at our specific examples, here's an overview of how fragmentation might manifest in the situations described.

Physical Fragmentation

- **Patchwork of Degradation.** The environmental impacts of mining, such as deforestation in Madagascar or soil erosion in India, create fragmented landscapes. This type of fragmentation affects biodiversity, disrupts ecosystems, and alters natural resources that communities depend on for other forms of subsistence. [Physical Fragmentation: Ecological]

Holistic Human Fragmentation

- **Health and Safety Risks.** Fragmentation in terms of health and safety practices means that some miners are exposed to high levels of risk, such as mercury exposure in Burkina Faso or unsafe tunnels in the DRC, with insufficient means to improve conditions, further dividing those able to work safely from those who cannot.

Societal Fragmentation

- **Artisanal and Small-scale Mining (ASM).** Each of these scenarios involves a significant amount of Artisanal and Small-Scale Mining (ASM), which is characterized by dispersed, informal operations rather than centralized, organized production. This leads to fragmented mining sites where consistency in methods, safety standards, and output quality can vary greatly. [Societal Fragmentation: Informational]

- **Lack of Regulation and Oversight**. In places like the DRC, India, and Burkina Faso, mining is often done without formal oversight, leading to fragmented regulation and enforcement. This makes it difficult to implement standardized practices across the industry. [Societal Fragmentation: Legal]

- **Inconsistent Policy Implementation**. Fragmentation at the governmental level, with inconsistent enforcement of mining regulations, results in uneven progress on environmental and social standards. Different regions may have varying levels of effectiveness in policy execution, contributing to a fragmented overall strategy for managing resources. [Societal Fragmentation: Legal]

- **Disparities in Revenue Distribution**. Although resource-rich, these regions often struggle with equitable distribution of wealth, leading to economic disparity. The profits gained from exports typically do not filter down to the local miners, creating a fragmented economic benefit structure where few reap substantial gains. [Societal Fragmentation: Economic]

- **Market Distribution**. These minerals feed into global supply chains that are often complex and fragmented, resulting in challenges in traceability and ensuring that profits do not contribute to conflict or are fairly distributed. [Societal Fragmentation: Economic]

- **Community Impact**. The reliance on mining can fragment communities, where socio-economic divides are exacerbated by the influx of wealth to a few and poverty for many. Child labor and the involvement of women in mining, as seen in these examples, can also lead to shifts and splits in traditional community roles and structures. [Societal Fragmentation: Social]

International initiatives, such as those promoting responsible mining and fair labor practices, aim to address these fragments by creating more cohesive systems of governance, regulation, and fair economic distribution. However, achieving uniformity in such complex scenarios remains a significant challenge, requiring collaboration across multiple sectors and levels of operation, especially in our increasingly disconnected global world.

But before delving more deeply into societal fragmentation let's further explore the holistic human fragmentation that is so prevalent in our tales from the mines.

Chapter 6
Holistic Human Fragmentation

The holistic human fragmentation domain encapsulates the intricate tapestry of experiences that define our lives, recognizing the profound interplay between mental, emotional, physical, and social dimensions. As we navigate an era marked by rapid technological advances and societal shifts, the need to understand and address the multifaceted nature of human fragmentation has never been more pressing.

This domain is crucial because it serves as the foundation from which all other domains of fragmentation emanate, human existence, impacting everything from how we interact with technology to how we form relationships and perceive our identities. It acknowledges that our mental health is intertwined with our emotional well-being, which, in turn, affects our physical health and safety. By understanding this interconnectedness, we gain deeper insights into the human condition and develop more effective means of fostering resilience and coherence in a fragmented world.

For instance, identity fragmentation can reverberate through cultural and societal structures, while cognitive fragmentation can shape how individuals engage with digital platforms or handle complex geopolitical realities. Likewise, trauma-induced fragmentation highlights the need for holistic recovery approaches that address both physiological and psychological aspects of trauma.

In essence, when addressing fragmentation the holistic human domain prompts us to view the human experience as a dynamic, interconnected whole. This perspective not only informs our approaches to personal and collective challenges but also inspires innovative solutions that honor the complexity of human life. By addressing the root causes of fragmentation within this domain, we can cultivate a more integrated, harmonious existence that respects the diverse realities of individuals across the globe.

There are seven types of fragmentation in this domain on which we will focus: identity, emotional, cognitive, trauma-induced, relational, behavioral, and health and safety.

Identity Fragmentation

Identity and self-perception involve how individuals understand themselves and their place in the world, encompassing roles, beliefs, values, and aspirations. A well-integrated sense of identity contributes to personal stability and confidence.

Identity fragmentation occurs when individuals face challenges in integrating various aspects of their identity. This can involve cultural, social, professional, or personal dimensions, particularly in diverse or shifting environments. Adults often encounter this fragmentation when adapting to new cultural settings, transitioning between professional roles, or balancing aspects of life that hold different values or expectations. This fragmentation can lead to identity crises, affecting self-esteem and well-being, as individuals struggle to form a cohesive self-concept. [*Reference:* Erikson, E. H. (1968). *Identity, Youth and Crisis.* Norton.]

The development of identity is a dynamic process that evolves over time. According to Erikson's theory of psychosocial development, individuals encounter specific identity-related challenges at different life stages, which can impact their self-perception and coherence. [*Reference*: Erikson, E. H. (1950). *Childhood and Society.* W.W. Norton & Company.]

In today's rapidly changing societal landscape, individuals might experience identity stress as they negotiate various, often conflicting, societal expectations and personal ambitions. The rise of social media can exert additional pressure on self-perception, as individuals constantly present curated identities online, potentially leading to fragmentation between one's private self and public persona. [*Reference:* Valkenburg, P. M., & Peter, J. (2011). Online Communication Among Adolescents: An Integrated Model of Its Attraction, Opportunities, and Risks. *Journal of Adolescent Health, 48*(2), 121-127.]

As an example of identity fragmentation, an adult living as an expatriate in a foreign country may struggle to integrate their cultural heritage with their new cultural environment. They may experience identity fragmentation as they try to balance their native traditions with those they encounter daily. [*Reference:* Benet-Martínez, V., Leu, J., Lee, F., & Morris, M. W. (2002). Negotiating biculturalism: Cultural frame switching in biculturals with oppositional vs. compatible cultural identities. *Journal of Cross-Cultural Psychology.*]

Addressing identity fragmentation involves fostering environments that support self-exploration and acceptance. Engaging in reflective practices, such as journaling and seeking feedback from trusted individuals, can aid in clarifying one's identity. Psychological interventions, including narrative therapy, can help individuals rewrite and integrate their life stories, enhancing their sense of coherence and self-understanding. Importantly, affirming one's core values and engaging in activities that align with those values can strengthen identity cohesion.

Identity fragmentation often intersects with societal cultural fragmentation when individuals navigate environments with distinct cultural divides or when cultural identity becomes a focal point in societal discourse. *Example:* An immigrant professional in a multicultural city might experience identity fragmentation while trying to integrate their ethnic identity with the dominant culture, exacerbated by societal tensions surrounding cultural integration.

Emotional Fragmentation

Emotional fragmentation is characterized by the experience of conflicting emotions that can be overwhelming and difficult to reconcile. It is a state where feelings are scattered and there is a lack of clarity or focus. This can manifest as difficulty concentrating [Societal Cognitive Fragmentation], emotional disconnection, or a fragmented sense of identity. [*Reference:* Siegel, D. J. (2010). *Mindsight: The New Science of Personal Transformation.* Bantam.]

As can be seen, the impact is often connected with cognitive and trauma-induced fragmentation. Causes may include stress, trauma, cognitive overload, or an inability to reconcile conflicting emotions or beliefs. Adults may encounter this type when faced with significant life changes, such as divorce, career shifts, or bereavement. In today's fast-paced world, people often experience cognitive overload due to constant information bombardment from multiple sources. This can lead to fragmented thinking, making it challenging to focus and prioritize tasks effectively. Emotional fragmentation can occur when individuals experience conflicting emotions or feel disconnected from their feelings, leading to challenges in managing their emotional well-being.

Studies suggest that emotional disconnection may serve as a protective strategy in the short term, helping individuals avoid overwhelming feelings. However, persistently relying on this disconnection can impede emotional regulation and lead to more significant mental health issues. [*Reference:* Tull, M. T., Stipelman, B. A., Salters-Pedneault, K., & Gratz, K. L. (2009). An examination of recent nonclinical panic: Its relation to emotion dysregulation, anxiety sensitivity, and experiential avoidance. *Journal of Anxiety Disorders, 23* (2), 303-311.]

Living in emotional disconnection can impact relationships, as emotional availability, empathy, and communication are crucial for meaningful connections. Individuals may struggle to communicate emotions or respond to others empathetically, leading to misunderstandings and strained interactions. Emotionally disconnected individuals might find themselves feeling isolated, even when surrounded by loved ones, as noted by Van Der Kolk, who argues that connection with others is integral to human experience. [*Reference:* Van Der Kolk, B. A. (2014). *The Body Keeps the Score: Brain, Mind, and Body in the Healing of Trauma.* Penguin Books.]

This fragmentation impacts mental health, contributing to issues like anxiety, depression, and stress. Individuals may feel overwhelmed by racing thoughts or trapped in negative emotional cycles, impacting their daily functioning and quality of life. To address mental and emotional fragmentation, practices such as mindfulness, therapy, and cognitive restructuring can help individuals regain clarity and focus. [*Reference:* Kabat-Zinn, J. (1994). *Wherever You Go, There You Are: Mindfulness Meditation in Everyday Life.* Hachette Books.]

Emotional Fragmentation

The struggle to navigate these fragmented emotions can hinder one's ability to process events healthily, potentially leading to emotional burnout or reduced emotional intelligence, which affects interpersonal relationships and decision-making. Daniel Goleman, a pioneer in emotional intelligence, argues that recognizing and managing one's own emotions is crucial for personal and professional success. He highlights that emotional fragmentation can be mitigated through developing strong emotional intelligence skills.

Building resilience through supportive relationships and seeking professional help when needed are also crucial strategies. Encouraging open communication about emotions, promoting mental health awareness, and creating supportive environments can enhance individual and collective well-being. Individuals can learn to integrate and harmonize their thoughts and emotions, leading to a more coherent sense of self and improved life satisfaction.

Addressing emotional disconnection involves therapeutic intervention, encouraging individuals to explore and reconnect with their emotions healthily. Approaches such as Cognitive Behavioral Therapy (CBT) and Dialectical Behavioral Therapy (DBT) can help in developing skills to understand and regulate emotions. Mindfulness practices also promote emotional awareness by encouraging individuals to observe and accept their emotions without judgment, thereby fostering a healthier emotional life. [*Reference:* Lineham, M. M (1993). *Cognitive-behavioral treatment of Borderline Personality Disorder.* Guilford Press.]

As an example of emotional fragmentation, a corporate executive may feel a combination of stress, satisfaction, and guilt over a high-stakes business decision that impacts employees' jobs. Managing these simultaneous, conflicting emotions can be overwhelming. [*Reference:* Mayer, J. D., & Salovey, P. (1997). What is emotional intelligence? In P. Salovey & D. Sluyter (Eds.), *Emotional Development and Emotional Intelligence: Educational Implications* (pp. 3-31). Basic Books.]

In countries experiencing significant political upheaval, like the United States amidst polarized governance, individuals often face emotional fragmentation. For example, consider a middle-class professional who fears the erosion of social safety nets such as social security or healthcare benefits. They may experience conflicting emotions of anxiety, anger, and helplessness as political decisions threaten their sense of stability and well-being. This fragmentation can lead to reduced emotional intelligence, impacting relationships and professional life. Without clear solutions to mitigate these fears, the individual could become isolated, turning to community activism or advocacy as a means to reclaim agency and find emotional coherence

Other Effects: Emotional fragmentation can be exacerbated by digital access fragmentation when disparities in digital connectivity limit access to mental health resources available online. *Example:* An adult living in a rural area with limited internet access may struggle to find online support groups or therapy, intensifying feelings of emotional isolation and fragmentation.

Cognitive Fragmentation

Cognitive fragmentation refers to a disruption in thought processes, often leading to disorganized thinking or compartmentalization. It occurs when an individual is exposed to too much information or too many demands on their attention and cognitive processing capacity, leading to a decreased ability to effectively process information or make decisions. This fragmentation can arise in high-stress environments or situations requiring multitasking.

In today's digital age, the constant influx of data from various digital devices, social media, and work demands can overwhelm our cognitive resources. This deluge of information can lead to feelings of stress, anxiety, and fatigue as the brain struggles to keep up with processing, sorting, and retaining what is relevant. Cognitive overload can detract from productivity and critical thinking, resulting in mistakes, decision fatigue, and impaired learning.

This phenomenon particularly impacts environments where multitasking is encouraged or required. Research by Adler and Benbunan-Fich highlights that multitasking can exacerbate cognitive overload, diminishing focus and reducing task efficiency. When faced with multitasking demands, individuals often switch attention rapidly between tasks, which can fragment cognitive processing and reduce performance quality on each individual task. This underscores the need for strategies to manage information flow and reduce cognitive burdens in both professional and personal settings.[*Reference:* Adler, R. F., & Benbunan-Fich, R. (2012). Juggling on a high wire: Multitasking effects on performance. *International Journal of Human-Computer Studies, 70* (2), 156-168.]

Howard Gardner's theory of multiple intelligences underscores how cognitive fragmentation might manifest when individuals are forced to work in areas misaligned with their natural cognitive strengths. Promoting diverse cognitive strengths can help mitigate fragmentation. [*Reference:* Gardner, H. (1983). *Frames of Mind: The Theory of Multiple Intelligences.* Basic Books.]

As an example of cognitive fragmentation, an adult entrepreneur juggling multiple business ventures might experience cognitive fragmentation that disrupts decision-making, leading to difficulties in prioritizing tasks effectively. [*Reference:* Diamond, A. (2013). Executive Functions. *Annual Review of Psychology, 64* , 135-168.]

Adaptation strategies are crucial for mitigating cognitive overload. Techniques such as mindfulness meditation can enhance an individual's capacity to manage stress and improve attention span. Furthermore, setting boundaries for digital consumption, prioritizing tasks, and scheduling breaks can help manage cognitive load effectively. Education systems and workplaces can also adopt processes that minimize unnecessary information overload and support focused engagement through more structured information delivery. [*Reference:* Zeidan, F., Johnson, S. K., Diamond, B. J., David, Z., & Goolkasian, P. (2010). Mindfulness meditation improves cognition: Evidence of brief mental training. *Consciousness and Cognition, 19* (2), 597-605.]

Cognitive fragmentation is often influenced by digital technological fragmentation, where incompatible technologies or multiple digital platforms overwhelm cognitive processing and focus. *Example:* A remote worker using various communication tools and platforms for tasks might experience cognitive fragmentation due to constantly switching contexts—hindering focus and productivity.

Trauma-Induced Fragmentation

Trauma-induced fragmentation results from traumatic experiences that lead to a compartmentalization of memories and emotions. This is often seen in adults who have endured significant trauma, such as combat veterans or survivors of abuse. It can manifest in dissociation, flashbacks, or emotional numbness, disrupting one's sense of self and ability to function. Understanding and addressing this type of fragmentation often requires therapeutic interventions to integrate fragmented memories and foster healing. Judith Herman, a renowned expert in trauma recovery, describes trauma as an experience that breaks the ordinary course of life. Successful therapy requires integrating these fragmented experiences into a cohesive narrative.

As an example of trauma-induced fragmentation, a veteran returning from combat faces trauma-induced fragmentation, struggling with flashbacks and fragmented memory recall related to their experiences in the field. [*Reference:* Herman, J. L. (1992). *Trauma and Recovery: The Aftermath of Violence— From Domestic Abuse to Political Terror*. Basic Books.] A fragmented mind in terms of memory gaps can occur regarding certain years of childhood, often related to traumatic events. [*Reference:* Van Der Hart, O., Niijenhuis, E. R. S., & Steele, K. (2006). *The Haunted Self: Structural Dissociation and the Treatment of Chronic Traumatization.* W.W. Norton & Company.]

As an example, let's briefly follow the story of Marcus … After surviving a devastating earthquake, Marcus found himself in a world that felt unfamiliar despite being in the same place he had spent his full life. The event had left not only his city in ruins but also fractured his sense of normalcy. On the outside, Marcus appeared to be coping, returning to work and resuming his daily routines. However, internally, he was navigating a fragmented landscape of emotions and memories. Everyday sounds, like passing sirens or even the rumble of a truck, triggered intense flashbacks. These episodes left him feeling disconnected from his own experiences, as if his body was on autopilot while his mind spiraled elsewhere. Seeking help, Marcus joined a support group where he learned to piece together his fragmented memories and emotions, gradually reconstructing a sense of safety and self-awareness in his rebuilt reality.

Other Effects: Trauma-induced fragmentation can compound health and safety fragmentation, affecting overall well-being and increasing vulnerability to physical and psychological risks. *Example:* A trauma survivor who experiences dissociative episodes may find it challenging to maintain daily routines that ensure their own health and safety, necessitating comprehensive therapeutic interventions.

Consider the experience of a civilian living in a region affected by ongoing conflict, such as Ukraine. The continuous threat of violence, displacement, and loss of loved ones can intensify trauma-induced fragmentation. This individual's daily life is fraught with flashbacks and anxiety, triggering a compartmentalization of memories where normalcy feels disrupted. As they attempt to navigate their shattered reality, personal identity may become intertwined with collective trauma, intensifying feelings of dissociation from both past and present. Such environments necessitate specialized therapeutic approaches that help in integrating these fragmented experiences into a resilient narrative of healing and adaptation.

Post-Traumatic Stress Disorder (PTSD) is a mental health condition triggered by experiencing or witnessing a traumatic event. It is characterized by a range of symptoms that can significantly impact daily functioning. These symptoms may include intrusive memories of the traumatic event, nightmares, and severe anxiety, as well as uncontrollable thoughts about the event. Individuals with PTSD might also experience emotional numbness, withdrawal from social interactions, and heightened reactions to situations reminiscent of the trauma. The disorder can affect anyone, regardless of age or background, and it often requires professional intervention such as therapy, medication, or support groups to manage and alleviate symptoms. Understanding PTSD is crucial not only for those affected but also for their friends and family, as support from loved ones plays a significant role in recovery. [*Reference:* American Psychiatric Association (2013). *Diagnostic and Statistical Manual of Mental Disorders* (5th ed.). American Psychiatric Publishing.]

Relational Fragmentation

Relational fragmentation emerges from difficulties in maintaining emotional connections and trust within relationships. Adults may face this when dealing with the fallout of broken relationships or when early attachment issues resurface in adult relationships. This fragmentation can create barriers to forming or sustaining meaningful connections, often leading to a cycle of isolation or repeated patterns of relational conflict, necessitating relational therapy or counseling to rebuild trust and connection. Brené Brown, known for her work on vulnerability and connection, emphasizes the importance of trust and empathy in overcoming relational fragmentation. Her research suggests fostering open communication to strengthen relationships. [Brown. B. (2012). *Daring Greatly: How the Courage to be Vulnerable Transforms the Way we Live, Love, Parent, and Lead.* Gotham Books.]

As an example of relational fragmentation, an adult who experienced emotional neglect in childhood might struggle to trust partners in romantic relationships, feeling isolated even when in the company of loved ones. [*Reference:* Mikulineer, M., & Shaver, P. R. (2007). *Attachment in Adulthood: Structure, Dynamics, and Change.* Guilford Press.]

Relational fragmentation can intersect with societal social fragmentation, where weakened community structures and networks amplify feelings of isolation in individual relationships. *Example:* During an urban crisis, such as a natural disaster, the breakdown of communal networks can deepen relational fragmentation for affected adults, increasing their sense of disconnection.

Behavioral Fragmentation

Behavioral fragmentation involves a disconnect between one's actions and personal values or beliefs, generating internal conflict. Adults frequently encounter this in scenarios where professional responsibilities conflict with personal ethics or when societal pressures challenge individual values. This fragmentation can lead to stress, decreased satisfaction, and a sense of inauthenticity, prompting the need for introspection and possibly behavioral therapies to realign actions with core values.

Internal Conflict

Albert Bandura's social cognitive theory emphasizes the role of self-efficacy in regulating behavior. He suggests that enhancing belief in personal effectiveness can reduce behavioral fragmentation by aligning actions with values. [*Reference:* Bandura, A. (1997). *Self-Efficacy: The Exercise of Control.* W.W. Freeman and Company.]

As an example of behavioral fragmentation, a professional may advocate for work-life balance at their company but find themselves unable to disconnect from work emails during personal time, experiencing tension between beliefs and actions. [*Reference:* Kegan, R., & Lahey, L. L. (2009). *Immunity to Change: How to Overcome It and Unlock the Potential in Yourself and Your Organization.* Harvard Business Press.]

Behavioral fragmentation may be influenced by digital regulatory fragmentation when cross-border digital policy differences hinder consistent ethical behavior across platforms. *Example:* An international businessperson might face ethical dilemmas due to varying data privacy laws, leading to behavioral fragmentation as they navigate compliance across jurisdictions.

Health and Safety Fragmentation

Health and safety fragmentation pertains to inconsistencies in maintaining physical, mental, and social well-being. For adults, the pressures of work-life balance, combined with health challenges can lead to neglect of personal well-being, increasing vulnerability to accidents or chronic conditions. Addressing this fragmentation emphasizes the importance of holistic health approaches, integrating mental health support, physical activity, and safety awareness to sustain well-being.

Michael Marmot, known for his work on social determinants of health, argues that socioeconomic factors such as status, education and environmental conditions play a significant role in health and safety fragmentation. Addressing these determinants can lead to improved holistic health outcomes. [*Reference:* Marmot, M. (2004). *The Status Syndrome: How Social Standing Affects Our Health and Longevity.* Henry Holt and Company.]

As an example of health and safety fragmentation, an office worker might feel pulled between pursuing a healthy lifestyle and coping with the stress of a demanding job, which could lead to neglecting personal health and well-being. [*Reference:* Siegrist, J. (1996). Adverse health effects of high-effort/low-reward conditions. *Journal of Occupational Health Psychology, 1* (1), 27-41.]

Making Connections

In addition to interactions across domains—highlighting the complexity and need for integrated approaches to addressing fragmentation—holistic human fragmentation encompasses various interrelated types within its domain, each reflecting distinct challenges but also revealing opportunities for comprehensive improvement. By examining these types comparatively, we recognize their entangled nature and can gain insights into the holistic approaches needed to address them effectively.

Identity vs Emotional Fragmentation. Identity fragmentation involves struggles with integrating various facets of self, often challenging one's self-concept and social belonging. Emotional fragmentation, on the other hand, is characterized by conflicting or disconnected emotions, impacting emotional intelligence. While identity fragmentation tends to focus on external influences and societal roles, emotional fragmentation deals more directly with internal emotional regulation. Both, however, can lead to a sense of instability that affects personal and interpersonal growth.

Cognitive vs Behavioral Fragmentation. Cognitive fragmentation disrupts coherent thought processes, affecting decision-making and focus, while behavioral fragmentation creates conflicts between actions and underlying values or beliefs. Cognitive fragmentation is often situational, influenced by external stressors or multitasking demands. Behavioral fragmentation can emerge from broader societal pressures or ethical dilemmas. Addressing one often leads to improvements in the other, as clearer thinking supports aligned actions.

Trauma-Induced vs Relational Fragmentation. Trauma-induced fragmentation stems from traumatic events leading to dissociation, while relational fragmentation arises from difficulties in forming and maintaining trust-based relationships. While trauma-induced fragmentation affects one's inner experiences and processing, relational fragmentation primarily impacts interpersonal dynamics. Nevertheless, both can feed into each other; unresolved trauma can hinder relationship-building, and unstable relationships can exacerbate feelings of isolation post-trauma.

Health and Safety Fragmentation. This type of fragmentation uniquely intertwines with all others, as it represents the well-being foundation encompassing physical, mental, and social health. Without stability in health and safety, efforts to address other fragmentation types may be compromised. Therefore, it's a crucial starting point for holistic interventions.

Addressing these fragmentations requires an integrated approach that considers the interconnectedness of human experiences. Holistic improvement emphasizes: (1) Interdisciplinary solutions (combining insights from psychology, sociology, technology, and health to tackle fragmentation comprehensively); (2) Therapeutic interventions (emphasizing therapeutic practices that integrate cognitive behavioral therapy, mindfulness, and community support systems); (3) Life balance and wellness initiatives (promoting work-life balance, stress management, and wellness programs to strengthen the health and safety framework); and (4) Community and social support (building strong community networks and fostering relational health to counteract the isolating tendencies of fragmentation types). Through this holistic approach, individuals can achieve greater coherence and resilience, transforming fragmentation into opportunities for growth and well-being enhancement.

Looking into the Future

The interplay among the types within this domain, and the other four domains—physical, digital, societal, and narrative and artistic fragmentation, will likely intensify as our world continues to rapidly fragment and evolve. *Fragmentation begets fragmentation.* Here's a future outlook on how these dynamics may unfold.

In the digital domain as technology becomes more embedded in our daily lives, we may face increasing cognitive and emotional fragmentation. However, advancements in artificial intelligence and digital platforms could also offer new tools for integration and coherence. Mindfulness apps, online therapy, and digital detox initiatives could become essential in managing the mental and emotional impacts of a hyper-connected world.

Globalization and cultural (societal) exchange will continue to blur traditional boundaries, potentially exacerbating identity fragmentation as individuals navigate multifaceted identities. In response, there might be a growing emphasis on cultural competence, identity education, and community-building initiatives that celebrate diversity and promote a cohesive sense of self within multicultural contexts. As societal structures evolve, relational fragmentation might increase due to changes in family dynamics, work environments, and community interactions. Future efforts may focus on fostering relational resilience through enhanced social networks, empathy training, and community support systems that emphasize the importance of connection and trust-building.

Health disparities and environmental challenges will likely intensify health and safety fragmentation. Future approaches may prioritize holistic health frameworks that integrate physical, mental, and social well-being, alongside policies that address social determinants of health to ensure equitable access to health resources and safe environments.

And as we seek meaning in an uncertain world, narrative/art fragmentation might become more pronounced, reflecting diverse and complex human experiences. This could lead to innovative storytelling and artistic expressions that both mirror and help alleviate the sense of fragmentation, providing pathways for shared understanding and empathy.

In Summary,

In this exploration of holistic human fragmentation, we dove into the multifaceted nature of human experiences in the context of modern life's rapid transformations and complexities. This chapter emphasizes the interconnectedness of mental, emotional, physical, and social dimensions, highlighting how fractures in this interconnectedness create distinct challenges across individual lives.

The chapter began by framing the importance of the holistic human domain—a foundational aspect that underlies broader fragmentation phenomena seen across various societal structures. From identity struggles faced by bicultural individuals to the emotional turmoil caused by digital access disparities, each type of fragmentation creates unique challenges that intertwine with other domains, including societal, digital, physical, and narrative/art environments. Recent global events, such as wars and political divisions, further amplify these fragmentation challenges.

We explored seven types of holistic human fragmentation: identity, emotional, cognitive, trauma-induced, relational, behavioral, and health and safety. For each type, the chapter provides not only theoretical grounding and illustrative examples but also narratives that concretize concepts. We observe, for instance, how civilians living in conflict zones, like Ukraine, endure trauma-induced fragmentation due to war, struggling to integrate fragmented memories and emotions amidst the chaos. Similarly, the political tearing apart of governments, as seen in polarized nations like the United States, fuels emotional fragmentation, leaving individuals grappling with anxiety and fear over the potential erosion of social safety nets.

These narratives illustrate how fragmentation impacts individuals' everyday lives—from professional dilemmas to coping with traumatic pasts and navigating political uncertainties. By understanding the depth and breadth of the holistic human fragmentation domain, we gain valuable insights for cultivating integrated solutions that honor the complexity of human life. We now delve into the digital fragmentation domain.

Chapter 7
Digital Fragmentation

In an era defined by unprecedented digital connectivity, the paradox of fragmentation permeates our technological landscape, posing profound implications for how we interact, govern, and innovate. Far from being technical inconveniences, these digital fractures echo the societal divides that have long challenged human progress. As we stand on the precipice of a new digital age powered by advances in artificial intelligence and networked technologies, understanding the multifaceted nature of digital fragmentation becomes imperative.

Imagine a world where your voice fades amidst clashing languages on the internet, or where the device you hold becomes obsolete overnight because of incompatible technologies. Picture entrepreneurs grappling with conflicting data regulations as they attempt to navigate international markets or the mounting frustration of communities that remain disconnected from the digital revolution sweeping across urban centers. These are not distant scenarios; they are the lived realities for millions today.

The digital world, often championed as the great equalizer, hides within its promise the grim truth of fragmentation—technological, regulatory, access, cultural/linguistic, platform, security, and economic. These fractures dictate who gets heard, who stays connected, and who prospers. As these digital divides widen, they threaten to solidify existing inequities, leaving behind those unable to keep pace with the relentless march of technological advancement.

Digital fragmentation—the splintering of digital systems and environment—is upon us. Let's explore more deeply some common types of digital fragmentation, each accompanied by examples.

Technological Fragmentation

Technological fragmentation arises from incompatible technologies and platforms. The pursuit of innovation, often led by market competition, results in distinct ecosystems. For instance, divergent operating systems such as Windows, macOS, and Linux necessitate separate development environments, complicating interoperability. Mobile platforms like iOS and Android further illustrate this, compelling developers to create different app versions, leading to siloed user experiences. Developers often need to create separate versions of their applications for each platform. AI and other rapidly evolving technologies compound these issues by regularly shifting technological standards and protocols. [*Reference:* Tyler, T. (2020). Mobile App Development: iOS vs. Android. *Digital Development Journal.*]

At the international level, different companies or countries might adopt incompatible technologies or standards, leading to an inability for systems to communicate effectively with each other. This can hinder innovation and collaboration across borders. Additionally, platform fragmentation occurs when software applications or services function differently on separate platforms or devices,, such as operation systems or browsers, requiring additional effort from developers to ensure compatibility.

As we have learned through the tales from the mines in Chapter 4, one area of fragmentation does not happen in isolation. How it influences other areas offers insights into the interconnected nature of modern challenges. Here's a look at the influence of technological fragmentation on:

- *Physical Fragmentation*: Fragmented technological ecosystems can lead to an increase in electronic waste, as devices and peripherals become obsolete or incompatible more quickly.
- *Holistic Human*: Users may experience frustration or stress due to frequent updates and the need to learn different systems, impacting their overall digital experience.
- *Narrative/Art*: Artistic and narrative expressions often explore themes of isolation and division caused by incompatible technologies, reflecting on the challenges of a disconnected digital world.
- *Societal Fragmentation*: Technological divides can exacerbate social inequalities, as access to certain technologies determines participation in various economic and educational opportunities.

Regulatory Fragmentation

As digital technologies become globally pervasive, regulatory fragmentation emerges from diverse national policies and regulations. Restrictions on data flow, local data storage requirements, or trade barriers can fragment the global digital economy, affecting everything from e-commerce to digital services.

The General Data Protection Regulation (GDPR) in Europe, juxtaposed against less stringent U.S. data protection laws, highlights how companies must navigate multiple frameworks to operate internationally, as briefly introduced above. Such complexities necessitate strategic physical infrastructure changes, like data center placement, to ensure compliance.

Variations in regulatory approaches can impede both international access and cooperation, impacting social cohesion and increasing operational costs for businesses. [*Reference:* Hoofnagle, C. J., van der Sloot, B., & Borgesius, F. J. Z. (2019). The European Union general data protection regulation: What it is and what it means. *Information & Communications Technology Law, 28*(1), 65-98.]

Here's a quick look at the influence of regulatory fragmentation on:

- *Physical Fragmentation*: Different regulatory environments can lead to physical infrastructure challenges, such as data centers being located strategically to comply with local laws.
- *Holistic Human*: Users may feel insecure about their data privacy due to differing regulations, leading to anxiety over information security.
- *Narrative/Art*: Stories and artworks often engage with the implications of surveillance and privacy, highlighting regulatory responses to digital realities.
- *Societal Fragmentation*: Varying regulations can create barriers to international collaboration, affecting global social cohesion and cooperation.

Access Fragmentation

Disparities in digital accessibility are manifestations of access fragmentation, often underpinned by socio-economic and geographic factors. The digital divide—particularly between urban and rural areas—limits internet connectivity and resources, perpetuating social inequalities. "Digital divide" refers to disparities between those with robust internet connectivity and digital literacy and those without. This divide can exacerbate existing social inequities, impacting education, economic opportunities, and social inclusion. Such fragmentation impedes infrastructure development in underserved areas, deepening isolation and exclusion from educational and economic opportunities. Technological advancements, though rapid, often fail to equitably bridge these divides due to uneven implementation.

Internet access varies greatly between urban and rural areas even in developed countries such as the United States, where rural communities often have less access to high-speed internet. [*Reference:* Whitacre, B. E., Gallardo, R., & Strover, S. (2014). Broadband's contribution to economic growth in rural areas: Moving towards a causal relationship. *Telecommunications Policy, 38* (11), 1011-1023.]

Digital Access Fragmentation

Further, censorship or blocking of websites and services in certain countries can fragment the internet experience for users, leading to isolated online environments.

Here's a quick look at the influence of access fragmentation on:

- *Physical Fragmentation*: Limited digital access impedes infrastructure development in underserved areas, perpetuating physical isolation.
- *Holistic Human*: A lack of access can lead to feelings of exclusion and disconnection for those unable to participate in digital spaces.
- *Narrative/Art*: : Artistic expressions may address themes of exclusion and the quest for connectivity in an increasingly digital world.
- *Societal Fragmentation*: It deepens the digital divide, creating disparate opportunities for education, employment, and social engagement across communities.

Cultural/Linguistic Fragmentation

The internet's predominantly English content exacerbates cultural and linguistic fragmentation, isolating non-English-speaking communities from global dialogues. This linguistic dominance marginalizes local cultures and diminishes cultural exchanges, impacting non-dominant language speakers' self-esteem and cultural identity. Despite technological advancements aiming for inclusivity, such as AI-driven translation tools, full cultural and linguistic integration remains elusive due to nuanced regional dialects and cultural contexts. Smaller markets with diverse languages, such as India, still face challenges in internet content accessibility and participation. [*Reference:* Harindranath, R., & Sein, M. K. (2007). Revisiting the role of ICT in development. *Proceedings of the 9th International Conference on Social Implications of Computers in Developing Countries.*]

Recent coordinated disinformation campaigns have targeted reputable news media, undermining their credibility and creating confusion among the public. Fragmented digital environments, emphasizing cultural and linguistic biases, often amplify these narratives. An instance includes concerted efforts to delegitimize trustworthy journalism regarding public health measures during the COVID-19 pandemic, where misinformation spread across fragmented platforms, contributing to public doubt and hindering coordinated public health responses.

Here's a quick look at the influence of cultural linguistic fragmentation on:

- *Physical Fragmentation*: Cultural and linguistic differences can lead to the physical preservation or marginalization of local cultures, as digital platforms prioritize dominant languages.
- *Holistic Human*: Non-dominant language speakers may feel marginalized, affecting their self-esteem and cultural identity.
- *Narrative/Art*: : Artworks often explore themes of cultural diversity and the tension between global and local identities in digital communication.
- *Societal Fragmentation*: Segmentation based on language affects community interactions and limits cultural exchange on a global scale.

A Story: Voices Across Boundaries

A young woman named Aisha, who lives in a small town in India, exemplifies the challenges of cultural linguistic fragmentation. Aisha is an enthusiastic and talented writer, penning her stories in her native language, Tamil. She dreams of sharing her perspectives with a global audience but finds herself constrained by the overwhelming dominance of English in the digital literary world.

Eager to connect with other writers, Aisha joins an international online writing forum. However, she quickly discovers that most discussions, resources, and networking opportunities are predominantly in English. Despite her proficiency in English, Aisha feels shy and reluctant to participate fully, worried her authentic voice might get lost in translation. The abundance of

English content and lack of recognition for her work in Tamil make her feel isolated, as if her stories held little value in the global scene.

This experience of cultural and linguistic fragmentation impacts Aisha on a personal level. Her self-esteem takes a hit, as she begins to question the worth of her cultural identity and the validity of her native language in a global context. She wonders if she needs to adapt her narratives to suit a more "universal" language to gain the recognition that feels out of reach.

On a societal level, the forum's predominantly English-speaking community misses out on the richness and diversity of stories like Aisha's that could broaden their perspectives. The digital platform inadvertently marginalizes non-English narratives, reinforcing a cultural hierarchy where only certain voices are amplified.

To navigate these challenges, Aisha decides to create a bilingual blog, where she publishes her stories in both Tamil and English. This allows her to maintain her cultural integrity while reaching a broader audience. Gradually, she connects with other writers from similarly diverse backgrounds, forming a sub-community within the larger forum that celebrates multilingualism and cultural exchange.

Aisha's story underscores the fragmentation caused by linguistic and cultural barriers, but it also illustrates resilience in overcoming these challenges. By embracing her own multicultural identity and language, she not only asserts her place in the global conversation but also contributes to a richer tapestry of global storytelling.

Platform Fragmentation

An explosion of digital platforms, each with distinct audiences and functionalities, illustrates platform fragmentation. Social media platforms like Facebook, X (formerly Twitter), and TikTok offer varied experiences, can isolate user interactions and data, leading to a fragmented digital experience where content and user engagement are contained within specific platforms Such fragmentation creates echo chambers, amplifying societal divisions and influencing public discourse.

For example, on social media platforms like Facebook and X, misinformation can rapidly proliferate within fragmented digital spaces due to algorithmically driven echo chambers. For instance, during election periods or health crises, false information campaigns often target these platforms to amplify distrust in official narratives and incite social unrest. This type of fragmentation allows misinformation to thrive unchallenged, weakening public trust and complicating efforts to present unified, fact-based discourses.

The pressure to maintain presence across multiple platforms can also lead to digital fatigue among users, affecting overall well-being and mental health. [*Reference:* Newman, N., Dutton, W. H., & Blank, G. (2012). Social Media in the Changing Ecology of News: The Fourth and Fifth Estates in Britain. *International Journal of Internet Science, 7* (1), 6-22.]

Here's a quick look at the influence of platform fragmentation on:

- *Physical Fragmentation*: Multiple platforms may lead to redundancy in resources and physical infrastructure to support different ecosystems.
- *Holistic Human*: Users may feel overwhelmed by the need to maintain presence across multiple platforms, leading to digital fatigue.
- *Narrative/Art*: : The distinctions between platforms inspire narratives about identity and interaction, often exploring the superficial nature of digital connections.
- *Societal Fragmentation*: Divided platforms create echo chambers, affecting social discourse and understanding across different groups.

Security Fragmentation

Variations in cybersecurity standards contribute to security fragmentation, with disparate levels of protection across networks and services. Secured platforms may not guarantee safe interactions with less secure counterparts, increasing vulnerabilities. This inconsistency can erode users' trust in digital environments, fostering anxiety about data privacy. Despite advancements in cybersecurity technologies, uneven implementation and lack of universal standards remain significant challenges.

Differences in cybersecurity infrastructure across industries and regions create significant security fragmentation. For example, financial institutions often implement robust cybersecurity measures, whereas other sectors, like small businesses or public institutions, may lack the resources for such defenses. This inconsistency leaves certain sectors more vulnerable to cyberattacks, like ransomware campaigns, impacting their trustworthiness and the security of user data. The recent surge in ransomware attacks on municipal infrastructure in small towns highlights this vulnerability, underscoring the need for comprehensive, cross-sector cybersecurity standards.

AI Dall-E's rendition of vulnerability and protection reflecting societal fears and narratives of security in the digital age.

Variability in cybersecurity measures can be seen in how different industries secure user data. For instance, financial institutions typically have more stringent security requirements compared to other sectors, leading to fragmented security standards. [*Reference:* Baer, W. S., & Parkinson, A. (2007). Cybersecurity and national policy. *Journal of Homeland Security and Emergency Management, 4* (2).]

Here's a quick look at the influence of security fragmentation on:

- *Physical Fragmentation*: Security measures may necessitate additional physical infrastructure, such as secure data storage facilities.
- *Holistic Human*: Concerns about security breaches and data privacy can cause anxiety and reduce users' trust in digital services.
- *Narrative/Art*: : Creative works often delve into themes of vulnerability and protection, reflecting societal fears and narratives of security in the digital age.
- *Societal Fragmentation*: Inconsistent cybersecurity standards can lead to unequal protection and trust in digital environments, impacting societal reliance on certain platforms.

Economic Fragmentation

Economic fragmentation highlights the inconsistencies in cybersecurity measures and standards across different digital systems and networks. Underscored by different pricing models and digital service costs, it compounds access disparities. For example, different pricing models and subscriptions for digital content and services create barriers for users from different economic backgrounds. This is evident in varying costs of digital services based on geographic location or currency strength.

The varying costs of streaming services exemplify economic fragmentation in the digital realm. Platforms like Netflix and Spotify adopt regional pricing models, which can limit accessibility based on the economic status of certain regions. For instance, while users in economically stronger regions may enjoy comprehensive service offerings at lower prices, those in developing countries might encounter higher relative costs for comparable content, exacerbating digital inclusion disparities and reinforcing global economic inequalities. [*Reference*: Lotz, A. D. (2017). Portals: A treatise on internet-distributed television. *Media Industries Journal, 4* (2), 35-47.]

Here's a quick look at the influence of digital economic fragmentation on:

- *Physical Fragmentation*: Economic barriers to access can limit the physical expansion of digital technologies and infrastructure in poorer regions.
- *Holistic Human*: A lack of access to affordable digital services can lead to feelings of resentment and frustration among economically disadvantaged groups.
- *Narrative/Art*: Economic disparities often inspire narratives surrounding equity and justice, drawing attention to the impact of economic barriers in digital fields.
- *Societal Fragmentation*: Economic fragmentation reinforces existing socio-economic inequalities, affecting access to digital resources and opportunities.

Consequences of Digital Fragmentation

The overall economic impact of digital fragmentation in today's global economy—regardless of the efforts of various autocratic leaders to expand borders and control the flow of information—can be daunting. Economically, fragmentation can lead to inefficiencies and increased costs for businesses that must adapt products and services to different standards or regulations. It can also stifle innovation by limiting access to global markets and collaboration opportunities.

In terms of interoperability, limited interoperability between digital systems can result in isolated data silos, hindering the flow of information and reducing the overall effectiveness of digital tools and services. Digital fragmentation can be a barrier to international collaboration and innovation, reducing the potential for global problem-solving through initiatives like open-source projects or international research partnerships.

Fragmentation due to restricted access to certain digital resources can lead to cultural isolation and limit exposure to diverse viewpoints and information, impacting societal development and understand. Even when digital connections through social media are consistently available, it's possible to experience digital fragmentation. Let's explore digital fragmentation from this point of view.

Users are often spread across a variety of social media platforms, each with its unique ecosystem, features, and communities (e.g., Facebook, Instagram, X, TikTok). This can lead to fragmentation as users engage predominantly within their chosen platforms, sometimes limiting cross-platform interactions. Further, different platforms may support different content formats or interaction styles, leading to a fragmented user experience where content might not be easily shared or understood across platforms.

In some regions, access to certain social media platforms may be restricted or censored, causing a fragmented digital experience where users in different parts of the world have limited communication or access to global conversations and networks. And diverse regulations regarding data use and privacy can fragment social media experiences, with companies often having different rules and features depending on regional legal requirements.

While social media creates opportunities for connection, a digital divide can still exist, as noted above. People without reliable internet access or digital literacy remain disconnected, leading to fragmentation in who can partake in digital interactions and to what extent. Further, language differences and cultural nuances can create fragmented communication, as users may gather in homogenous groups, limiting exposure to diverse perspectives.

Social media platforms use algorithms to personalize content feeds, often creating echo chambers where users are exposed primarily to information that aligns with their interest or beliefs. This can fragment public discourse and reduce exposure to broader viewpoints. Therefore, while social media connects individuals globally, fragmentation can still occur at technological, regulatory and social levels, affecting how people interact and perceive the digital landscape.

In Summary,

As we navigate the complexities of the 21st century, digital fragmentation emerges not just as a consequence of technological advancement but as a defining issue that shapes every facet of our lives. It serves as a poignant reminder that the digital realm, with all its promise, is intrinsically linked to the social, economic, and cultural fabric of society. This interconnectedness demands our attention, for in every fragmented digital experience lies the potential to both reflect and magnify broader societal divides.

One crucial aspect of digital fragmentation is the pervasive issue of misinformation, exacerbated by the rapid dissemination capabilities of digital platforms. The fragmentation of digital platforms leads to echo chambers where misinformation spreads unchecked, often amplified by algorithms designed to prioritize engagement over accuracy. For instance, echo chambers on platforms like Facebook and X facilitate the spread of misinformation during critical times, such as elections and health crises, undermining public trust and credible journalism.

This challenge is exemplified by recent attacks on the news media, where fragmented platform ecosystems have allowed false information to proliferate, undermining public trust in credible journalism. For instance, during recent global events such as elections and public health crises, we've seen how misinformation can cloud public perception and influence outcomes. A notable example involves coordinated disinformation campaigns targeting news outlets, questioning their integrity and credibility, leading to widespread distrust. This situation illustrates how platform fragmentation, combined with cultural and linguistic biases in content algorithms, can erode a foundational pillar of informed democracy.

In this age of rapid technological evolution, artificial intelligence and digital platforms wield unprecedented influence, touching everything from our personal interactions to global economic structures. They challenge us to rethink how we approach access, regulation, cultural exchange, and the dissemination of information. There's an urgent need to reevaluate strategies to ensure these platforms uphold principles of accuracy and reliability, fostering inclusivity and coherence.

The true test of our digital future lies in our ability to bridge these divides, bringing unity and cohesion, fostering environments that promote cooperation, understanding, and equitable access. It requires transforming digital challenges into opportunities for change, where misinformation is met with robust factual counter-narratives and where media literacy becomes integral to digital engagement.

The prevalence of digital fragmentation is intricately linked to rapid technological progression, regulatory complexities, and socio-economic disparities. Addressing these challenges, alongside the critical issue of misinformation, requires collaborative efforts among technology developers, policymakers, civil society, and global organizations. Together, they must strive to create cohesive and inclusive digital environments, emphasizing interoperability, equitable access, unified regulatory frameworks, and enhanced media literacy to foster a more connected and integrated global community.

By acknowledging and addressing the myriad ways in which digital fragmentation intersects with other domains and challenges like misinformation, we can lay the groundwork for a more unified and resilient global society. The call to action is clear. We need to harness the power of technology not just for innovation's sake, but to build bridges across these digital chasms, creating a world where every voice is heard, every community connected, and every individual empowered.

Chapter 8
Narrative/Art Fragmentation

In an era where rapid technological and societal changes continually reshape our world, narrative and art stand as pivotal pillars that both reflect and influence the human experience. Far beyond simple forms of entertainment or aesthetic expression, they serve as vital conduits for empathy and understanding, bridging diverse perspectives and fostering deeper insights into the complexities of modern life. As the stories we tell and the art we create navigate through fragmented realities, they offer profound opportunities to challenge assumptions, illuminate hidden truths, and promote a collective awakening to the nuanced layers of our global existence.

This chapter delves into the vibrant interplay of narrative and art fragmentation, illustrating how structural, temporal, thematic, visual, character, and linguistic fragmentation reveal the intricacies of our lived experiences. Through evocative descriptions of artwork and narrative examples, we explore the compelling ways that fragmentation prompts both creators and audiences to engage with the world innovatively. By referencing these diverse forms of fragmentation, this chapter invites us to actively piece together and derive meaning, highlighting art's and narrative's power to transform and connect disparate elements of human experience within our shared and fragmented reality.

Narrative and art fragmentation, though often viewed as challenges, can catalyze innovation in how we perceive identity, culture, and technology. By embracing the multifaceted ways in which stories and artworks are produced and consumed across various media and contexts, we expand our capacity to engage with the world. This ongoing dialogue between creators and audiences encourages us to explore the unseen, question norms, and ultimately, cultivate a more inclusive and empathetic society.

As we delve deeper into the nuances of narrative/art fragmentation, we uncover its essential role in shaping our understanding of reality, highlighting its power to open minds and bridge disparate worlds within our shared human experience.

While narrative/art fragmentation can be both intentional (fragmentation created by choice) and accidental/incidental (not created by choice), just as other domains and types of fragmentation, it also has the potential of being contextual, collaborative, and technological. These additional contexts illustrate that fragmentation can emerge in diverse ways across different creative processes and environments.

Contextual context happens when external factors, such as cultural shifts or historical context, change how a work is perceived over time, leading to new interpretations that fragment the original narrative. For example, a classic novel might be fragmented in its interpretation when readers from different eras or cultural backgrounds apply contemporary lenses to its themes and characters.

Collaborative context occurs in works created by multiple contributors who may have different visions or styles, leading to a naturally fragmented narrative or artwork. For example, an anthology with stories from different authors that presents a varied or fragmented thematic structure due to diverse voices.

Collected works or collaborative contexts are an important aspect of 21st-century business books. In today's uncertain and rapidly changing interconnected world, businesses face complex challenges that require diverse perspectives and innovative solutions. By incorporating multiple contributors with different visions and expertise, business books can offer a more comprehensive and multifaceted understanding of key issues.

Further, such collections can introduce readers to a wide range of ideas and strategies, enriching their knowledge and helping them to think more creatively. This diversity in thought can lead to more adaptive and inclusive solutions, which are crucial in a globalized market. Moreover, collaborative works can expose readers to varying cultural and industry-specific insights, thereby broadening their perspectives and enhancing their ability to engage with diverse teams and markets effectively. Overall, embracing diverse voices in business literature not only reflects the complexity of modern challenges but also equips leaders and organization with the tools to navigate then successfully.

Technological context is when modern technology introduces fragmentation, such as when digital media are presented in various formats or platforms, altering the experience of the narrative. An example is a multimedia project that includes video, text, and interactive elements might result in a more fragmented narrative experience depending on how each medium is consumed.

There are six types of fragmentation in the narrative/art domain serving various purposes such as reflecting the complexity of reality, engaging the audience actively in interpretation, or exploring modernist and postmodernist themes. These fragmentations are structural, temporal, thematic, visual, character, and linguist. They challenge traditional perceptions of coherence and unity in storytelling and art.

Structural Fragmentation

This involves breaking up the linear or coherent structure of a narrative or artwork, often presenting disjointed or non-sequential events and pieces. It challenges the viewer or reader to assemble the narrative themselves. *Example:* Novels like "Infinite Jest" by David Foster Wallace, which use footnotes and multiple storylines to create a complex, non-linear narrative structure.

Art Fragmentation:

Art Description: The artwork presents a chaotic city skyline, mosaic-like in appearance, where buildings of different architectural styles from various eras are juxtaposed. These structures—ranging from ancient remnants to contemporary facades and futuristic abstracts—interlace in a disordered array, with bridges and elevated walkways leading to unexpected places. The sky above, segmented with contrasting colors and weather patterns, adds dissonance to this visual symphony.

Demonstration of Fragmentation: Structural fragmentation is evident in the non-linear arrangement of city elements, providing no single coherent vantage point. The viewer must engage actively, navigating through the architectural cacophony to construct a personal interpretation of the cityscape, mirroring the fragmented structure.

Narrative: "Windwood"

The village of Windwood was known for its peculiar tales, but none so enigmatic as the saga of the lost heirloom. Rather than unfolding in a traditional manner, the story scattered itself across fragments, much like the ancient map that purportedly led to the treasure.

Part I: A letter, yellowed with age, discovered under the floorboards of the old Windwood Inn. It speaks of a ruby pendant, passed down through generations, its last known location described in cryptic verses: "Where shadows play at break of day, beneath the whispering oak."

Part VII: In a dusty library, a diary entry dated decades later describes a young boy's adventure through the village fields. He speaks of hidden caves and enigmatic stone circles, hinting at secrets buried where the earth meets the forest edge.

Interlude: A newspaper clipping surfaces, detailing the gala at Windwood Hall—a night when the pendant was last seen. The column, scattered with reports of laughter and scandal, leaves readers wondering about the night's true events.

Epilogue: A faded photograph in the attic, capturing a group of villagers by the river. Labeled only with a date, it reveals in the background what appears to be a glint of red, nearly lost to time—a whisper of the heirloom's presence.

Fragmented like a puzzle, these pieces float through Windwood's history, each offering a glimpse yet never a complete picture. The villagers exchange stories, assemble parts, and challenge assumptions, attempting to weave coherence from the disjointed tales. In doing so, they create countless versions of the narrative, each adding to the vibrant tapestry of Windwood lore.

Narrative Description: The story of Windwood involves the mysterious saga of a lost heirloom, delivered in fragmented forms such as a letter, a diary entry, a newspaper clipping, and a photograph.

Demonstration of Fragmentation: This narrative structure is non-linear, with pieces such as letters, diary entries, clippings, and photographs scattered across different forms and time periods. Readers must actively piece together the various elements to form a coherent picture of the story. The disjointed structure challenges traditional storytelling by requiring the reader to assemble the narrative themselves from the fragmented clues provided.

Temporal Fragmentation

This type involves the disruption of time flow within a narrative or artwork, such as flashbacks, flash-forwards, or a non-cohesive timeline. *Example:* Films like *Memento*, where the story unfolds in reverse chronological order, engaging the audience in piecing together the timeline

Art Fragmentation:

Art Description: This painting depicts a singular tree in a field, its branches capturing distinct moments in time simultaneously: spring's green, summer's bloom, autumn's fiery tones, and winter's bare branches. The sky is an amalgam of day and night hues—dawn's pinks, midday's brightness, sunset's gold, and night's starry navy—reflecting a non-linear passage of time.

Demonstration of Fragmentation: Temporal fragmentation disrupts the conventional flow of time by presenting multiple seasons and times of day in one scene. Viewers are prompted to consider the fluidity of time, as the artwork invites them to perceive multiple temporalities as part of a grander, continuous narrative.

Narrative: "Clara's Manor"

In the old manor on the edge of town, time seemed to spiral rather than march. Clara, drawn to its mysteries, discovered that each room carried the echo of a different era.

Stepping into the sunlit parlor, she immediately found herself amidst a vibrant 1920s gathering. The room was alive with jazz music flowing from a gramophone, and flapper dresses swirled around her. Clara could almost taste the Prohibition-era champagne, though she knew it would vanish once she left the room.

Venturing down the dim corridor, she pushed open another door and was met with the stillness of the 1850s. Dust motes hovered in the stale air, and the walls whispered stories of civil discourse and handwritten letters left unsent on the mahogany desk. The scent of candle wax and distant wars lingered.

In the attic, Clara encountered the echoes of a future not yet known. Holoscreens shimmered beside repurposed antiques, and children's laughter mingled with digital chimes. Here, technological marvels existed side-by-side with remnants of what was, or might be.

The garden was a collision of seasons, where roses bloomed alongside snow-covered paths—a space outside of linear time, where nature danced to its own rhythm, unaffected by the constraints inside the manor.

Clara found her way to the library at the heart of the house, where journals and diaries from every era were scattered across tables. Here, past and future existed in parallel, each page a portal to a different moment in time. She picked up a diary from 2099, its ink still fresh, narrating thoughts not yet formed.

As night enveloped the manor, Clara understood the enchantment of temporal fragmentation. The house was a living mosaic of time—a place where history, present, and future interwove, inviting her to piece together the narrative and find her place within its timeless embrace.

Narrative Description: Clara explores a manor where different rooms and spaces each represent a different era, from the 1920s to an unnamed future, causing time to be experienced non-sequentially.

Demonstration of Fragmentation: The narrative disrupts the conventional flow of time, presenting moments from the past, present, and future as coexisting yet separate experiences. This fragmentation engages the reader in navigating through different temporal layers simultaneously, emphasizing the interplay and fluidity of time. Each space within the manor offers glimpses of past, present, and future, creating a rich tapestry that invites exploration and interpretation.

Thematic Fragmentation

This involves exploring disparate or contrasting themes within a single work, which might not straightforwardly connect but create a rich tapestry of ideas. *Example:* The works of artist Jean-Michel Basquiat, which often juxtapose themes of race, identity, and history in non-linear and fragmented ways.

Art Fragmentation:

Art Description: A collage juxtaposes elements emblematic of different themes: industry with factories and machinery, nature with vivid landscapes, and personal identity with intimate portraits. Abstract symbols and text, like snippets of poetry or headlines, weave across these disparate scenes, representing communication and media.

Demonstration of Fragmentation: Thematic fragmentation is portrayed through the juxtaposition of contrasting themes within the same visual space. This structure forces viewers to make connections and explore the interplay and conflict between industrialization, natural beauty, and personal identity, revealing complexity within the supposedly compartmentalized ideas

Narrative: "Seabrook"

In the small coastal town of Seabrook, life unfolded like the tides—restless, rhythmic, and full of secrets. The townsfolk knew each other by name, but beneath polite conversations lay unspoken stories, each anchored in different realities.

In the morning, the smell of salt and seaweed mingled with fresh-baked bread as Emma, the baker's daughter, crafted loaves while daydreaming of distant places. Her corner of Seabrook brimmed with themes of tradition and longing. The bakery's warmth contrasted with her yearnings for adventure, both comforting and confining.

At the edge of town, the lighthouse stood as a beacon, not just guiding ships but serving as a canvas for the hidden artist Tobias. With each splash of paint, he wrestled with chosen themes of solitude and creation, leaving mirrors of his heart on crumbling walls. Art was his refuge, yet each brushstroke spoke to isolation and silent screams for connection.

Down by the docks, old fishermen spun tales of storms weathered and harvests gathered, their narratives dipped in perseverance and survival. Their stories, shared over mugs of ale, held lessons in resilience, coloring the air with the scent of salt and smoke—themes of life's harshness and its unexpected beauty intertwined.

On Wednesdays, Seabrook's chapel became a symphony hall, echoes of hymns mingling with Nick's guitar melodies. His music blurred sacred and secular, weaving themes of faith and doubt into a single thread—a quest for understanding beyond mere belief, searching for a divine tune in everyday dissonance.

As the day faded to dusk, the fragments of Seabrook's essence came alive under a shared sky, individual themes intersecting like waves in the harbor. In the reflective stillness, each soul pondered their chosen paths, embracing the thematic fragments of their lives that, when knit together, formed the evolving tapestry of Seabrook's existence.

Narrative Description: The town of Seabrook showcases varied individual themes through its residents' lives—tradition, creation, resilience, and faith.

Demonstration of Fragmentation: This narrative utilizes thematic fragmentation by weaving disparate themes—tradition and longing, solitude and creation, resilience and beauty, faith and doubt—each represented by different characters and settings within the town of Seabrook. These themes, while individually divergent, invites readers to explore the rich tapestry of contrasting themes, reflecting the complexity and richness of human experience.

Visual Fragmentation

In visual arts, this involves the use of disjointed, abstract, or collage-like elements that fragment the visual field, requiring the viewer to piece together meaning from seemingly unrelated parts. *Example:* Cubism, as seen in Picasso's works, where objects are broken up into geometric shapes and reassembled in abstract forms.

Art Fragmentation:

Art Description: An abstract piece uses numerous geometric shapes and patterns that intersect wildly. Each fragment hosts different colors and art styles, such as smooth gradients alongside harsh lines, each housing seemingly isolated images—a realistic eye, a fabric swatch, a map piece.

Demonstration of Fragmentation: Visual fragmentation emerges through the lack of conventional cohesion, as the abstractly arranged fragments demand viewers' active engagement to discern meaning. The disjointed images compel viewers to explore potential relationships among the disparate pieces, enhancing interpretive depth.

Character Fragmentation

This occurs when characters in narratives are intentionally presented in fragmented or contradictory ways, reflecting complex or conflicting facets of their personalities. *Example:* Characters in Virginia Woolf's *Mrs. Dalloway* are presented with internal monologues that reveal fragmented and diverse aspects of their inner lives.

Art Fragmentation:

Art Description: A complex portrait of a single figure composed of overlapping facial sections, each with divergent expressions and styles. One segment is serene and pastel-colored; another is fiery with bold strokes; a third is whimsical and surreal, each hinting at different facets of the character's identity.

Demonstration of Fragmentation: Character fragmentation is highlighted through the portrayal of multifaceted identities within one person. Through this mosaic, viewers encounter the diverse and possibly conflicting aspects of the character, reflecting the non-uniform nature of human identity and sparking introspective thought on the fragmented self.

Narrative: "Alex's Identities"

In the heart of the city, where the old clock tower cast long shadows across cobblestone streets, Alex stood still, feeling the hum of life pulse around him. He wore a knowing smile, or was it weariness? It depended on who observed.

In the mornings, Alex was Adrian—meticulous and calculated, gliding through the financial district in tailored suits. His colleagues knew him as the strategist, the steady hand, who turned numbers into stories of triumph. Yet, amid boardroom victories, Adrian often glimpsed another self-reflected in paneled glass.

By afternoon, as the sun dipped behind skyscrapers, Alex let the artist emerge. Under the pen name Aiden, he slipped into bustling cafés, sketchpad in hand, capturing the nuances of human emotion with sprawling strokes of ink. Some recognized Aiden as the dreamer, whose gallery openings whispered of brilliance tinged with melancholy.

Evening shadows beckoned Augustine. The philosopher, perched by the window of his book-filled apartment, absorbed in volumes of history and existential musings. Augustine shared his thoughts as fragments of essays scattered in obscure journals, pondering the tangles of identity—a dialogue with himself across the spectrums of time and thought.

On weekends, when whim and fancy dictated, Alex embraced Austin— the friend who danced through parks with light-hearted laughter, spinning tales from nothing and everything, breaking into spontaneous adventures with a ragtag crew who valued spontaneity over structure.

Each aspect of Alex, a lens through which the world was understood and articulated, existed harmoniously yet separately, like separate pages in an unfinished novel. Individually fragmented but collectively coherent, the facets combined to create a tapestry that was Alex, each telling a part of an ever-evolving story.

Under the clock tower's watchful gaze, he reflected on the intersections and departures of his identities, pondering if each audience saw truth or merely a version. With a resolute step, Alex carried them all forward, each fragment shaping the narrative of his singular, multifaceted life.

Narrative Description: Alex embodies multiple identities—Adrian, Aiden, Augustine, and Austin—each engaging with the world in distinct ways.

Demonstration of Fragmentation: This narrative showcases character fragmentation by illustrating Alex's distinctly separate identities, each with its own attributes and environments. These varied personas interact with the world in unique ways, presenting a complex tapestry of a single individual whose fragmented characters together enrich his overall narrative. The reader is encouraged to explore the multifaceted nature of identity and how disparate elements may coexist within a single individual.

Linguistic Fragmentation

This involves the use of fragmented language, syntax, or dialogue to create a sense of chaos or disconnection within a narrative. *Example:* The style of James Joyce's *Finnegans Wake*, which employs inventive, fragmented language that challenges conventional reading.

Narrative: "Evelyn's Market"

In the dim glow of streetlights, Evelyn navigated the bustling market square, a cacophony of voices echoing in her mind like an orchestra tuning up. Her thoughts drifted in and out of coherence—fluttering memories, broken syntax, and vivid imagery colliding without warning.

Through the crowd, she caught snippets of languages she barely recognized, words hanging in the air like autumn leaves caught in a whirlwind. "Bonjour... delayed sunrises," a voice whispered, fading into "una sombra de lo que fue... the whispering past."

Evelyn paused before a fruit stall, its display a sensory jumble—golden oranges, crimson apples, and the scent of fresh basil mingling with distant laughter. "Apples remind me of... childhood," she mused, recalling sunlit kitchens and her grandmother's gentle hums.

Turning away, she was swept into a kaleidoscope of sights and sounds. Signs painted with bright colors screamed for attention—SALE! 节日快乐 !عروض خاصة! Each demanded different fragments of memory and understanding, creating a montage of past travels and old friends.

Her phone buzzed, jolting her back to the moment. A text from her brother: "Got the postcard. Sea forever, was it Cheshire or Venice?" She laughed softly, the question disjointed but familiar, like a family secret half-remembered.

As dusk settled, Evelyn wandered toward the riverbank, her mind a tapestry of fragmented dialogue and emotion. The narrative flowed and ebbed like the water at her feet—a poetic mélange of languages, colors, and echoes, weaving her past with the present.

Narrative Description: Evelyn walks through a market square where her internal monologue, mixed languages, and sensory experiences collide, creating a fragmented narrative.

Demonstration of Fragmentation: This narrative uses fragmented language—disjointed language and syntax—to reflect Evelyn's scattered thoughts and perceptions, creating a fluid, dream-like atmosphere. The disjointed dialogue and shifting imagery reflect the protagonist's internal and external experiences, mirroring the chaos and diversity of language and experience, requiring readers to piece together and construct meaning from the linguistic and sensory fragments presented.

Narrative/Art Impact on Other Fragmentation Domains

Narrative and art fragmentation can influence other types of fragmentation in various ways. Here's how it can impact physical, holistic human, digital, and societal fragmentation, with examples for each.

Physical Fragmentation. *Impact:* Fragmented narratives and art can influence how physical spaces are designed or perceived, often reflecting or inducing disjointedness in real-world environments. *Example:* Urban art installations that deliberately fragment space, such as Olafur Eliasson's works, challenge viewers to experience and interpret spaces differently. His "Weather Project" at Tate Modern, with its vast installation obscuring parts of the Turbine Hall, alters perception and interaction with the physical space.

Holistic Human Fragmentation. *Impact:* Fragmented narratives and art can resonate with or even contribute to mental and emotional fragmentation by reflecting complex emotional states or psychological experiences. *Example:* The film *Eternal Sunshine of the Spotless Mind* employs a fragmented narrative structure to depict the process of erasing memories of a past relationship. The disjoined storyline mirrors the protagonists' emotional fragmentation as they struggle to reconcile their feelings and experiences.

Digital Fragmentation. *Impact:* Fragmented narratives in digital formats can contribute to digital fragmentation by requiring audiences to engage with multiple platforms to access the full story, affecting how digital content is consumed. *Example:* The storytelling of transmedia franchises like *Star Wars*, where books, games, and films contribute to the overarching narrative, reflects digital fragmentation. Each medium presents fragmented information that fans piece together to understand the entire story universe.

Societal Fragmentation. *Impact:* Art and narrative fragmentation can mirror or critique societal fragmentation, often highlighting inequalities, diverse perspectives, or social divides. *Example:* The novel *Invisible Man* by Ralph Ellison uses a fragmented narrative to explore themes of racial identity and invisibility in society. It reflects societal fragmentation by illustrating the protagonist's disjointed experiences and struggles within a racially divided society.

These examples show that narrative and art fragmentation can profoundly impact various facets of real-world fragmentation, illustrating their interconnectedness and the potential for art to reveal and influence broader societal and personal dynamics.

Fragmentation in Narratives

The concept of fragmentation in narratives and art often emerges from broader discussions on literary theory, art criticism, and cultural studies rather than being rigidly categorized. However, exploring these themes through existing scholarly works can provide valuable insights into how fragmentation operates across different contexts. By drawing from theories of narrative structure, media studies, and cross-cultural analysis, one can better understand how and why fragmentation is used or occurs both intentionally and incidentally.

Narrative structure theories explore how stories are organized and how their elements interact to create meaning. Fragmentation within narrative structure breaks away from traditional linear storytelling, offering opportunities to explore non-linear plots, multiple perspectives, and incomplete narratives that engage the audience actively. This approach foregrounds the reader or viewer's role in piecing together the story.

Seymour Chatman's work delves into how narrative components—such as plot, time, and perspective—can be manipulated, providing insights into how fragmented narratives challenge and engage audiences by requiring them to reconstruct the story's events and themes. [*Reference:* Chatman, S. (1978). *Story and Discourse: Narrative Structure in Fiction and Film.* Cornell University Press.]

Example: Consider a novel like *Cloud Atlas* by David Mitchell. The book consists of six interconnected stories set across different times and places, each fragment told in a distinct style. The narrative structure is purposefully fragmented, with stories presented as nested and discontinuous narratives that echo and contrast with one another. This challenges readers to piece together the overarching narrative and themes about interconnectedness and human experience.

Media studies examine how different media and technologies shape the way content is created, distributed, and consumed. With the advent of digital media, fragmentation becomes a central feature of contemporary storytelling. Multiple platforms and formats can deliver fragmented narratives, each contributing a piece to the overall story and influencing how audiences engage with the content.

Bolter and Grusin discuss the notion of remediation, where new media refashions older media forms. This process inherently involves fragmentation, as elements are adapted for different formats, creating diverse and non-linear narrative experiences across media platforms. [*Reference:* Bolter, J. D., & Grusin, R. (2000). *Remediation: Understanding New Media* . MIT Press.]

Example: The film *The Matrix* and its associated media ecosystem offer a prime example. The narrative is fragmented across movies, animated shorts (*The Animatrix*), video games, and comics. Each medium provides different perspectives and pieces of the overarching story, requiring audiences to consume multiple formats to fully understand the complexities of the narrative world, reflecting media studies' emphasis on multilinear storytelling enabled by modern technology.

Cross-cultural analysis focuses on how cultural contexts influence the interpretation and creation of narratives and art. Fragmentation in this domain can emerge from cultural exchanges or contrasts, where differing traditions, values, and historical contexts intersect, resulting in hybrid or fragmented representations.

Homi Bhabha's seminal work explores concepts like hybridity and the "third space," where cultural meanings are negotiated and redefined. Fragmentation occurs as elements from different cultures are juxtaposed, creating narratives and artworks that reflect complex, multifaceted identities. [*Reference:* Bhabha, H. K. (1994). *The Location of Culture*. Routledge.]

Example: The novel *Americanah* by Chimamanda Ngozi Adichie explores themes of immigration, identity, and cultural fragmentation. The story follows Ifemelu, a Nigerian woman living in the U.S., as she navigates her identity across different cultural landscapes. The narrative reflects cross-cultural fragmentation as Ifemelu reconciles her Nigerian heritage with her American experiences, offering readers insights into the complexities of cultural hybridity and identity negotiation.

These stories exemplify how fragmentation can be employed across different theoretical perspectives to enrich narrative complexity and thematic depth, engaging audiences in uniquely challenging and insightful ways

In Summary ...

As we reach the end of this exploration into narrative and art fragmentation, we reflect on the multifaceted ways in which these phenomena challenge and enrich our understanding of the human experience. Through detailed descriptions of artwork and narratives, we've delved into how structural, temporal, thematic, visual, character, and linguistic fragmentations serve as powerful tools for both creators and audiences.

We've seen how structural fragmentation invites us to piece together disjointed elements, creating coherence from chaos. Temporal fragmentation disrupts linearity, allowing us to experience the fluidity of time. Thematic fragmentation challenges us to connect seemingly disparate ideas, enriching our appreciation of complex themes. Visual fragmentation engages us in active interpretation, assembling meaning from abstract elements. Character fragmentation reveals the multifaceted nature of identity, encouraging introspection and empathy. Meanwhile, linguistic fragmentation reflects the rich diversity of language and communication, highlighting the intricacy of human thought and expression.

Through these examples, we have learned that fragmentation is more than disruption. It is an avenue for deep engagement, reflection, and creativity. It compels us to navigate our fragmented world with curiosity and openness, embracing the potential for innovation and connection. As artists, storytellers, and audience members, we are reminded of our role in shaping and interpreting these narratives, fostering a more inclusive and empathetic society. Ultimately, fragmentation proves to be a lens through which the complexity and beauty of our shared human experience can be better understood and appreciated.

Chapter 9
Societal Fragmentation

The landscape of societal fragmentation is complex. Multiple factors intersect, influencing the social fabric and cohesion of communities at local, national, and global levels. Understanding these dynamics is crucial for addressing issues related to social integration and equity, which, regardless of the current political trend to ignore them, will inevitably surface in the global world in which we play a role.

Societal fragmentation refers to the division and disconnection within a society, often resulting in reduced social cohesion and increased disparities among groups. The wealthier get wealthier; the poorer grow poorer. Social fragmentation occurs when divisions within a community or society become pronounced, often manifesting through differing beliefs, values, practices, or identities.

This fragmentation can arise from a variety of sources, including political, economic, cultural, and technological factors. Different beliefs, values or practices can lead to a lack of unity. Disparities in wealth and access to resources can create social divides leading to fragmented communities. Diversity in race, religion, language, and identity, while enriching, can also lead to fragmentation if not embraced inclusively. Increasing division in political beliefs and ideologies can exacerbate societal fragmentation, often fueled by media and political rhetoric. And the rapid pace of technological advancement and influence of social media can create echo chambers, reinforcing existing beliefs and isolating groups from diverse perspectives.

Institutions play a pivotal role in both mitigating and exacerbating societal fragmentation across economic, cultural, political, social, religious, informational, and legal domains. As the foundational structures within which interactions occur, institutions have the power to foster inclusivity and cohesion or reinforce existing divides. Economic institutions, such as financial systems and regulatory bodies, can either promote equitable access to resources or deepen economic disparities. Cultural and educational institutions help shape societal values and norms, acting as bridges or barriers to cultural integration. Political institutions govern resource distribution and representation, influencing the degree of political fragmentation. Social institutions, including family and community organizations, determine the strength of community ties. Religious institutions can promote peace across faiths or intensify sectarian divides. Media and information institutions regulate the flow of information, impacting the extent of informational fragmentation. Lastly, legal institutions uphold the rule of law, influencing the consistency and fairness of legal protections and obligations. Understanding the role of institutions is crucial for addressing societal fragmentation, as they are instrumental in shaping the social fabric and promoting resilience and cohesion.

In a world that is more interconnected than ever, the threads of our social fabric are constantly tested by the forces of division and disconnection. Societal fragmentation presents itself in many forms, subtly weaving its way into our lives through economic disparities, cultural divides, political polarization, and more. These seemingly disparate strands shape our everyday experiences, influencing our interactions, beliefs, and opportunities. As we navigate this complex landscape, understanding the multifaceted nature of societal fragmentation becomes crucial. It invites us to examine not just the challenges it presents, but also the potential pathways to greater unity and resilience. Together, let's uncover the intricate dynamics that define our world today.

DALL-E rendition of societal fragmentation.

Economic Fragmentation

Economic fragmentation occurs when disparities exist within or between regions, sectors, or groups, often leading to uneven development and inequality. This fragmentation can manifest in various forms, such as urban-rural divides, technological versus traditional industries, and income inequality among different demographic groups. Disparities in economic resources and access to opportunities can create tension and instability as wealth becomes concentrated in certain areas while others are neglected or declines. In the United States, income inequality has led to distinct lifestyles and opportunities for the wealthy compared to lower-income communities, contributing to stratification in housing, education, employment opportunities, and healthcare. [*Reference:* Piketty, T. (2014). *Capital in the Twenty-First Century.* Harvard University Press.]

Technological advancements can contribute to economic fragmentation, as industries and individuals unable to keep pace with digital transformations may fall behind. This digital divide impacts employment and productivity, as well as social equity, further entrenching inequality. For instance, access to high-speed internet and digital skills becomes crucial in a technology-driven economy, leaving rural areas and older workers at a disadvantage. [*Reference:* Stiglitz, J. E. (2012). *The Price of Inequality: How Today's Divided Society Endangers Our Future.* W. W. Norton & Company.]

Globalization has both exacerbated and ameliorated economic fragmentation. On one hand, it can lead to disparities between developing and developed nations, as wealth and resources are disproportionately allocated. On the other hand, trade and international cooperation can drive economic growth and reduce poverty if managed equitably. Addressing economic fragmentation involves fostering inclusive growth policies, investing in infrastructure, education, and technology, and implementing measures to ensure fair distribution of wealth and opportunities.

International cooperation, sustainable economic development practices, and policies focused on reducing barriers to entry for disadvantaged groups or regions are essential. Mechanisms like social safety nets, targeted investments in education and technology, and support for industries in transition can help mitigate the adverse effects of economic fragmentation. Building a more inclusive economy ensures that growth benefits are shared widely and contribute to overall social and economic stability. [*Reference:* Piketty, Thomas (2014). *Capital in the Twenty-First Century.* Harvard University Press.]

Societal economic fragmentation has a strong relationship with other areas of fragmentation. Related to *physical fragmentation*, economic   disparities often lead to the development of segregated urban areas, with wealthier communities having better infrastructure and amenities, while poorer areas may suffer from neglect and decay, further physically fragmenting urban landscapes. Related to *digital fragmentation*, economic inequality can cause a digital divide, where lower-income populations have less access to technology and the internet, leading to unequal participation and representation in the digital space.

Related to *holistic human fragmentation*, economic disparities can contribute to stress and anxiety, affecting mental health and leading to mental/emotional fragmentation as individuals experience varying levels of access to mental health resources. Further, economic inequalities are often reflected in *art and media*, where stories and representations highlight the disparity between different economic classes and their respective struggles.

Cultural Fragmentation

Cultural fragmentation is the division of society along cultural or ethnic lines, leading to distinct communities that maintain separate traditions, languages, or cultural identities. In Belgium, an example is the linguistic and cultural divide between the Flemish-speaking region of Flanders and the French-speaking region of Wallonia where cultural and linguistic differences have led to political and social tensions. [*Reference:* Sinardet, D. (2010). Belgium's "Impossible" Biculturalism: Between Cultural Diversity and Federalist Consensus. *Social Compass, 57* (2), 227-236.]

Cultural and ethnic diversity, while enriching, can lead to fragmentation if not managed inclusively. Societies that do not embrace pluralism risk marginalizing minority groups, leading to social tensions and conflicts. Political polarization further deepens societal divisions, with media and technology amplifying differences rather than promoting understanding. This can weaken democratic processes, as dialogue becomes contentious and consensus harder to achieve.

Societal cultural fragmentation has direct ties to other areas of fragmentation. Related to *physical fragmentation*, cultural divisions can influence residential segregation, where different cultural or ethnic groups cluster in specific neighborhoods, leading to distinct physical separations within cities and regions. Related to *digital fragmentation*, cultural fragmentation can result in language barriers and cultural differences online, creating isolated digital communities that engage primarily with culturally specific content.

Related to *holistic human fragmentation*, cultural tensions can result in language barriers and cultural differences online, creating isolated digital communities that engage primarily with culturally specific content. Further, cultural fragmentation inspires diverse *narratives and art* that explore themes of identity, belonging, and multiculturalism, sometimes leading to fragmented storytelling styles that reflect varied cultural perspectives.

Political Fragmentation

Political fragmentation refers to the division of society based on divergent political beliefs and ideologies, which can lead to polarized communities and gridlock in governance. A political system where multiple parties, factions, or interest groups operate with conflicting goals or ideologies can lead to instability, as forming cohesive policies or governments becomes challenging. For instance, coalition governments may struggle to find common ground if fragmented parties pursue divergent agendas. Such fragmentation can also weaken governance, as legislative gridlock may arise when competing factions are unable to reach consensus on critical issues, delaying decision-making and policy implementation.

Moreover, political fragmentation can lead to increased polarization, where political debates become more about opposing ideologies than constructive dialogue. Such is the case in the United States, where distinct and opposing views between Republicans and Democrats have led to societal division and challenges in passing bipartisan legislation. [*Reference:* Fiorina, M. P., & Abrams, S. J. (2008). Political Polarization in the American Public. *Annual Review of Political Science, 11* , 563-588.]

This divisiveness can hinder democratic processes, where citizens feel alienated from the political system that appears incapable of addressing their needs effectively. The lack of a dominant party or coalition often results in short-term governance focused more on maintaining power than achieving long-term solutions. In extreme cases, this can destabilize governments, leading to frequent elections or changes in leadership, which disrupts continuity and progress. [*Reference:* Lipset, S. M. (1960). *Political Man: The Social Bases of Politics*. Doubleday & Company, Inc.]

Fragmentation also poses risks for national stability as it can exacerbate underlying social divisions. When political parties align themselves along ethnic, regional, or religious lines, the fragmentation deepens societal divides. It risks marginalizing certain groups and may lead to social unrest or conflict, as seen in several multi-ethnic nations. Conversely, political fragmentation can sometimes foster diversity and representation, giving minority voices a platform, but this potential benefit is often outweighed by the challenges it imposes on unity and effective governance.

Addressing political fragmentation requires deliberate efforts to promote dialogue and cooperation among diverse political entities. Electoral reforms, like ranked choice voting or proportional representation, can help facilitate broader representation without resulting in excessive fragmentation. Effective leadership is essential, as it requires bridging divides and fostering an environment where compromise and collaboration are valued over confrontation and division. Emphasizing shared national goals and identity can help counteract divisive forces within the political landscape. [*Reference:* Liiphart, A. (1999). *Patterns of Democracy: Government Forms and Performance in Thirty-Six Countries.* Yale University Press.]

The relationship of societal political fragmentation to the other domains of fragmentation is as follows: In terms of *physical fragmentation*, political differences can create physical divides, such as protests or clashes in certain areas, leading to visible geographical separations based on political affiliations. In relationship to *digital fragmentation*, political polarization can contribute to digital echo chambers, where individuals only engage with like-minded communities, intensifying digital fragmentation. In relationship to *holistic human fragmentation*, political tensions may cause stress and anxiety, impacting individuals' mental health as they navigate polarized environments and contentious political discourses. And politically charged *art and narratives* reflect polarized views, often addressing themes of division and ideological conflict.

Social Fragmentation

Social fragmentation is the breakdown of social networks and community structures, leading to isolation and weakening of communal ties. In urban areas like Los Angeles, the phenomenon of isolated "gated communities" can contribute to social fragmentation, as residents have limited interactions with broader neighborhood communities. [*Reference:* Blakely, E. J., & Snyder, M. G. (1997). *Fortress America: Gated Communities in the United States.* Brookings Institution Press.]

Societal social fragmentation relates to other domains of fragmentation as follows. In terms of *physical fragmentation*, social isolation can influence how communities are physically structured, with gated neighborhoods or separated communities highlighting social divides. In relation to *digital fragmentation*, social fragmentation might lead to digital spaces mirroring real-world social segregation, where communities interact within closed digital networks.

In relation to *holistic human fragmentation*, social isolation can exacerbate mental health issues, leading to feelings of loneliness and disconnection from society at large. And *artistic works* often explore themes of alienation and connection, reflecting the impact of social fragmentation on personal and collective narratives.

Religious Fragmentation

Religious fragmentation involves divisions within society based on religious beliefs and practices, which can lead to separate communities defined by distinct religious identities. For example, in Nigeria tensions between the predominantly Muslim-majority North and the Christian-majority South often highlight issues of religious fragmentation, shaping socio-political dynamics which influence social policies and inter-communal relations. [*Reference:* Falola, T., & Heaton, M. M. (2008). *A History of Nigeria* . Cambridge University Press.]

In relationship to *physical fragmentation*, religious divides can manifest in segregated living areas, where different religious communities settle in distinct geographical regions. In relation to *digital fragmentation*, online spaces may reflect religious divisions, with communities forming around shared religious beliefs and content, sometimes leading to insular digital networks. In relation to *holistic human fragmentation*, religious fragmentation can lead to identity struggles and exclusion, impacting individuals' mental and emotional well-being. In relation to *narrative/art fragmentation*, religious themes in art and storytelling often explore differences and commonalities between faiths, occasionally highlighting divisions and shared human experiences.

Informational Fragmentation

This is the division within society based on access to and consumption of different sets of information, often leading to contrasting world views or understandings of reality. An example is the phenomenon of "echo chambers" on social media platforms such as Facebook, where algorithms promote content that reinforces users' existing beliefs, contributing to informational fragmentation. [*Reference:* Sunstein, C. R. (2017). *Republic: Divided Democracy in the Age of Social Media*. Princeton University Press.]

Information fragmentation has been exacerbated by the wide use of misinformation and disinformation. This contributes to informational fragmentation by distorting the landscape of information that people consume. Misinformation refers to the spread of false or misleading information without harmful intent, while disinformation is the deliberate dissemination of false information with the intent to deceive. Both phenomena can polarize societies by creating competing narratives and worldviews, making it difficult for individuals to discern facts from falsehoods.

This fragmentation occurs because misinformation and disinformation often reinforce pre-existing biases and beliefs, leading to the formation of echo chambers where individuals are only exposed to information that aligns with their views. Social media platforms, with their algorithms prioritizing engaging content, can amplify these misleading narratives, isolating people from diverse perspectives. As a result, communities become ideologically separated, making consensus and productive dialogue more challenging to achieve. [*Reference:* Bennet, A., & Turner, R. (2023). *Reblooming the Knowledge Movement: The Democratization of Organizations.* MQIPress.]

In a variety of ways, informational fragmentation is intertwined with all domains of fragmentation. In relation to *physical fragmentation*, disparate access to information can physically manifest in regions where knowledge and education infrastructure are unevenly developed, leading to physical divides in educational facilities and opportunities. In relation to *digital fragmentation*, information divides create echo chambers and reinforce digital fragmentation, affecting how communities interact and share knowledge. In relation to *holistic human fragmentation*, limited access to diverse information can reinforce narrow worldviews and contribute to emotional strain, especially when confronted with opposing perspectives. Further, disparate access to information can lead to fragmented storytelling, where *narratives* reflect the isolated perspectives shaped by informational echo chambers.

Legal Fragmentation

Legal fragmentation involves discrepancies and variations in the enactment, interpretation, and enforcement of laws across different jurisdictions or regions. This form of fragmentation may lead to inconsistencies in legal protections and obligations, potentially impacting access to justice and fostering inequality.

In federated systems like the United States, legal fragmentation can occur when federal and state laws conflict, or when different states have divergent legal standards on topics such as cannabis legalization or healthcare. This results in people facing different legal landscapes simply based on geographic location, impacting mobility and equity. [*Reference*: Gerken, H. K. (2017). Federalism as the new nationalism: An overview. *Yale Law Journal, 123*, 1889-1935.]

In the U.S., during the past two administrations, continuous legal fragmentation has occurred as both elected and non-elected politicians have engaged in vexatious litigation. This entails repeatedly bringing frivolous lawsuits solely to harass, subdue, or punish an adversity. This also includes the use of delay tactics, submitting unnecessary rebuttals and motions intended to overwhelm the opposing party and prolong legal proceedings rather than resolve a legitimate legal issue.

The rule of law is a foundational principle that underpins a fair and just society, where *every individual, institution, and government entity is accountable to laws* that are publicly promulgated, equally enforced, and independently adjudicated. It ensures that *no one is above the law* and that legal rights are protected in a consistent and transparent manner. The rule of law promotes equality by guaranteeing that laws are applied impartially, protecting citizens from arbitrary governance and abuse of power. It fosters trust within society, as individuals are assured that their rights and responsibilities are predictable and stable, encouraging investment and participation in civic life. Moreover, the rule of law supports the functioning of democratic systems by upholding the integrity of legal processes and ensuring that justice is accessible to all, thereby contributing to social stability and economic development.

The concept of the rule of law is deeply rooted in legal philosophy and is referenced across numerous legal and academic texts. A key reference often cited in discussions about the rule of law is A.V. Dicey's work, *Introduction to the Study of the Law of the Constitution* (first published in 1885), which outlines the core principles of the rule of law. Dicey emphasized the importance of legal equality and the predominance of legal reasoning over arbitrary power.

Another significant reference is Fuller's *The Morality of Law*, which discusses the procedural aspects necessary to uphold the rule of law. Additionally, various international documents, such as the *Universal Declaration of Human Rights* and the *United Nations Charter*, underscore the rule of law as essential for global governance and human rights protection. These texts and frameworks collectively shape the understanding and application of the rule of law in various legal contexts. [*Reference*: Fuller, L. L. (1964). *The Morality of Law*. Yale University Press.]

The effects of legal fragmentation are closely linked to other domains of fragmentation. In relation to *physical fragmentation*, legal inconsistencies can lead to geographic divides where people relocate to regions with more favorable legal conditions, further entrenching socio-economic and cultural divisions. In relation to *informational fragmentation*, varying legal standards can contribute to confusion and misinformation about legal rights and responsibilities, complicating effective information sharing across regions.

In terms of *digital fragmentation*, access to legal resources and understanding of rights may vary greatly, with some groups having limited exposure to necessary legal assistance or education, reinforcing digital divides. In relation to *holistic human fragmentation*, disparities in legal protections can foster feelings of injustice and marginalization, impacting individual and community trust in the system.

Lastly, in terms of *narrative/art fragmentation*, differing legal landscapes can inspire artistic explorations of justice, rights, and identity, reflecting societal debates on fairness and equality. These narratives can illuminate both the struggles and resilience of communities navigating fragmented legal realities.

In Summary ...

As we have explored, societal fragmentation manifests through various dimensions such as economic inequality, cultural divides, political polarization, and more. These divisions do not exist in isolation; they intricately interweave, affecting communities at every level. Economic fragmentation, for instance, influences access to resources and opportunities, often exacerbating social and cultural divisions. Similarly, digital and informational fragmentation not only shape how we consume information but also impact our perceptions and interactions, further deepening existing divides. Understanding these dynamics is crucial, as they directly affect the cohesion and stability of societies.

Moreover, while fragmentation brings unique challenges to social integration and equity, it also presents opportunities for reflection, dialogue, and reform. By acknowledging the varied expressions of fragmentation, we can work towards policies and practices that promote inclusivity and resilience. Whether through fostering cultural understanding, addressing economic disparities, or reforming political systems, addressing these fragmentations requires a multifaceted and collaborative approach. We will explore this more deeply in the coming chapters.

As we move forward, the erosion of trust emerges as a crucial issue intertwined with fragmentation, impacting the very fabric of our social structures and relationships. Trust is the connective tissue that binds societies together, and examining how fragmentation contributes to its erosion will be essential in charting a course toward a more cohesive and equitable future.

Chapter 10
The Erosion of Trust

Trust is the cornerstone of democracy. It's the foundation upon which democratic institutions and processes are built, playing a crucial role in the functioning and stability of any democracy. When citizens trust their government and institutions, they are more likely to participate in the democratic process, comply with laws, and support public policies. Here are a few key reasons why trust is essential in a democracy:

1. **Legitimacy**: Trust in democratic institutions and processes provides legitimacy to the government and its actions. When people believe in the integrity and fairness of elections and other democratic mechanisms, they are more likely to accept the outcomes, even if those outcomes don't align with their personal preferences.

2. **Social Cohesion**: Trust fosters social cohesion by creating a sense of community and shared purpose. It helps bridge divides and enables citizens to work collectively to address common challenges. [*Reference:* Fukuyama, F. (1995). *Trust: The Social Virtues and the Creation of Prosperity.* Free Press.]

3. **Effective Governance**: Trust between citizens and government officials facilitates cooperation and dialogue, making it easier to implement policies and achieve societal goals. It encourages compliance with laws and regulations, reducing the need for coercive enforcement measures.

4. **Civic Engagement**: Trust boosts civic engagement by motivating individuals to participate in political and community activities. When people trust that their voices will be heard, they are more likely to vote, join civic groups, and engage in public discussions. [*Reference:* Hardin, R. (2006). *Trust.* Polity.]

5. **Resilience**: Democracies with high levels of trust tend to be more resilient in the face of crises. Trust builds a reservoir of goodwill that can sustain democratic norms and values even during challenging times.

Trust and Fragmentation

Trust, once a binding agent in the socio-political fabric, is now frequently at risk, tested by the increasing fragmentation within and among democratic institutions. This fragmentation not only weakens governance but also erodes the public's faith in the very systems designed to represent and protect them. Let's briefly take a look at the fragmentation effect impact on trust from the viewpoint of high-level aspects of society.

Aspect	Fragmentation Effect	Impact on Trust
Social Cohesion	Fragmentation in societal groups and communities.	Trust among individuals and groups diminishes, leading to increased polarization. [*Reference:* Coleman, J. S. (1990). *Foundations of Social Theory.* Harvard University Press.]
Market Dynamics	Fragmented markets with varied regulations and standards.	Consumer and investor trust can be eroded due to uncertainty and instability. [*Reference:* Fukuyama, F. (1995). *Trust: The Social Virtues and The Creation of Prosperity.* Free Press.]
Information Flow	Fragmentation in media and communication channels.	Trust in information accuracy declines, fostering misinformation and skepticism. [*Reference:* Giddens, A. (1990). *The Consequences of Modernity.* Polity Press.]
Organizational Structure	Fragmented organizational hierarchies or divisions.	Trust in leadership and decision-making processes can weaken due to lack of unified direction. [*Reference:* Kahleer, M., & Lake, D. A. (Eds.) (2003). *Governance in a Global Economy: Political Authority in Transition.* Princeton University Press.]
Cultural Unity	Fragmentation across cultural or ethnic lines.	Social trust decreases, leading to tensions and potential conflicts. [*Reference:* Putnam, R. D. (2000). *Bowling Alone: The Collapse and Revival of American Community.* Simon & Schuster.]
Supply Chains	Fragmented supply chain processes and logistics.	Trust in product quality and supply reliability is compromised, affecting consumer confidence. [*Reference:* Christopher, M. (2016). *Logistics and Supply Chain Management* (5th ed). Pearson.]

The current crisis of trust and fragmentation in democracies is not without historical precedent. Putnam traces the decline of social capital in the United States over several decades, linking it to broader societal changes. Understanding this historical context is crucial for several reasons. First, it reminds us that democracies have faced and overcome challenges to trust before. Second, it helps identify long-term trends that contribute to fragmentation, such as changes in media consumption, declining civic engagement, or shifting economic structures. Finally, historical analysis can reveal successful strategies from the past that might be adapted to address current challenges to democratic cohesion. [*Reference:* Putnam, R. D. (2000). *Bowling Alone: The Collapse and Revival of American Community*. Simon & Schuster.]

The challenges of trust and fragmentation are not uniform across democracies. Dalton provides a comparative analysis of political support erosion in advanced industrial democracies, highlighting how different political cultures and institutional structures can influence patterns of trust and fragmentation. For instance, consensus-based political systems might experience different dynamics of fragmentation compared to majoritarian systems. Similarly, countries with strong traditions of civil society might show more resilience in the face of fragmentary pressures. [*Reference:* Dalton, R. J. (2004).. Oxford University Press. *Democratic Challenges, Democratic Choices: The Erosion of Political Support in Advanced Industrial Democracies.*]

Understanding the delicate interplay between trust and fragmentation is crucial for diagnosing the challenges currently facing modern democracies like the United States, and for seeking pathways to restore faith in these foundational institutions.

Social Division and Fragmentation. Fragmentation often stems from increasing social divisions [societal social fragmentation], where diverse groups within society find themselves at odds over economic, cultural, or political matters. This division creates competing narratives and diminishes common ground, leading to mistrust among citizens. The trust erosion manifests through skepticism about whether democratic institutions serve all equally or merely cater to certain factions.

Putnam argues that increasing diversity in societies can lead to reduced social trust and cohesion in the short term. This aligns with the observation that fragmentation often stems from increasing social divisions, where diverse groups within society find themselves at odds over economic, cultural, or political matters. These divisions create competing narratives and diminish common ground, leading to mistrust among citizens and skepticism about whether democratic institutions equally serve all. [*Reference:* Putnam, R. D. (2007). E pluribus unum: Diversity and community in the twenty-first century. *Scandinavian Political Studies, 30*(2), 137-174.]

Digital Democracy and Trust. The digital age has introduced new dimensions to democratic participation and trust. Margetts and colleagues explore how social media and other digital platforms shape collective action and political engagement. While these technologies offer new avenues for civic participation and can increase transparency, they also present challenges [digital fragmentation]. [*Reference:* Margetts, H., John, P., Hale, S., & Yasseri, T. (2015). *Political Turbulence: How Social Media Shape Collective Action*. Princeton University Press.]

The ease of spreading misinformation online (see below) can exacerbate fragmentation and erode trust. Moreover, the digital divide can create new forms of exclusion. However, e-governance initiatives and online platforms for citizen engagement also offer opportunities to rebuild trust by making government more accessible and responsive. The challenge lies in harnessing the positive potential of digital democracy while mitigating its fragmentary effects.

Media Influence and Misinformation. The role of media—traditional and digital—cannot be overlooked when discussing trust and fragmentation [societal informational fragmentation]. Media not only shapes public perception but often amplifies divisive rhetoric. With misinformation circulating more freely, it further fractures societal trust in legitimate news sources and institutional truth. These rifts contribute to a fragmented society unable to unite behind shared facts or purposes.

Vosoughi and colleagues demonstrate that false information spreads more rapidly and broadly on social media platforms than truthful information. This proliferation of misinformation further fractures societal trust in legitimate news sources and institutional truth, contributing to a fragmented society unable to unite behind shared facts or purposes. [*Reference:* Vosoughi, S., Roy, D., & Aral, S. (2018). The spread of true and false news online. *Science, 359*(6380), 1146-1151.]

Political Polarization. Partisan divides enhance societal political fragmentation, with political allegiances overshadowing national or communal identities. As political parties become more ideologically extreme, the electorate mirrors this polarization, leading to gridlock and a lack of trust in the government's ability to act efficiently and justly. In this case, voters perceive democratic institutions as being co-opted by partisan interests rather than being impartial arbiters of the public good.

Iyengar and his colleagues argue that political polarization is driven more by emotional attachments to parties than by ideological differences. This affective polarization contributes to partisan divides that enhance fragmentation, as political allegiances overshadow national or communal identities. The result is often gridlock and a lack of trust in the government's ability to act efficiently and justly. [*Reference:* Iyengar, S., Sood, G., & Lelkes, Y. (2012). Affect, not ideology: A social identity perspective on polarization. *Public Opinion Quarterly, 76*(3), 405-431.]

Economic Disparities. Economic inequality is a potent driver of distrust and fragmentation [societal economic fragmentation]. When a significant portion of the population feels left behind economically, it can suspect that the system favors the wealthy or privileged. This perception exacerbates divides, creating an "us vs. them" mindset that further fragments societies.

Piketty and Saez provide evidence of long-term trends in economic inequality. When a significant portion of the population feels left behind economically, it can suspect that the system favors the wealthy or privileged. This perception exacerbates divides, creating that "us vs. them" mindset mentioned above. [*Reference:* Piketty, T., & Saez, E. (2014). Inequality in the long run. *Science, 344*(6186), 838-843.]

Cultural Shifts. As societies become more diverse, cultural clashes can arise, challenging long-standing norms and values [societal cultural fragmentation]. This cultural flux can lead to fragmentation when certain groups feel their way of life is under threat. Without robust frameworks for dialogue and inclusion, such tensions can deepen, fostering environments ripe for distrust.

Inglehart and Norris discuss how cultural backlash against progressive values has contributed to the rise of populist movements. As societies become more diverse, cultural clashes can arise, challenging long-standing norms and values. This cultural flux can lead to fragmentation. [*Reference:* Inglehart, R., & Norris, P. (2017). Trump and the populist authoritarian parties: The silent revolution in reverse. *Perspectives on Politics, 15*(2), 443-454.]

Institutional Failures. Fragmentation is often exacerbated by perceived or real institutional failures [societal legal fragmentation]. Scandals, corruption, and inefficacy within government entities can greatly undermine public trust. When institutions fail to deliver justice or transparency, they become fragmented from the populace they are meant to serve.

Rothstein and Teorell define quality of government as the impartiality of institutions that exercise government authority. Deviations from this impartiality, such as scandals, corruption, and inefficacy within government entities, can greatly undermine public trust. When institutions fail to deliver justice or transparency, they become fragmented from the populace they are meant to serve. [*Reference:* Rothstein, B., & Teorell, J. (2008). What is quality of government? A theory of impartial government institutions. *Governance, 21*(2), 165-190.]

It's crucial to distinguish between institutional trust and social trust when examining fragmentation in democracies. Uslaner defines institutional trust as confidence in government bodies, media, and other formal structures, while social trust refers to the faith citizens have in one another. He argues that generalized social trust is more fundamental and harder to change than institutional trust. [*Reference:* Uslaner, E. M. (2002). *The Moral Foundations of Trust*. Cambridge University Press.]

In fragmented societies, we often see a decline in both forms of trust, but they can erode at different rates and for different reasons. For instance, a scandal might quickly diminish institutional trust, while the erosion of social trust tends to be a slower process linked to broader societal changes. Understanding this distinction is key to developing targeted strategies for rebuilding trust in fragmented democracies.

Trust, the Cornerstone of Democracy

Global Influences. In an interconnected world, international dynamics can impact domestic trust. Global challenges like climate change, migration, and economic shifts may fragment trust if citizens believe their country's response is inadequate or misaligned with global trends.

Kriesi and his colleagues examine how globalization impacts national politics, potentially leading to fragmentation and new political cleavages. In an interconnected world, international dynamics can impact domestic trust. Global challenges like climate change, migration, and economic shifts may fragment trust if citizens believe their country's response is inadequate or misaligned with global trends. [*Reference:* Kriesi, H., Grande, E., Lachat, R., Dolezal, M., Bornschier, S., & Frey, T. (2006). Globalization and the transformation of the national political space: Six European countries compared. *European Journal of Political Research, 45*(6), 921-956.]

Erosion of Trust in the United States

Alex's father, William Demetrious Sioris, spent his life honoring and loving the United States of America. Leaving his homeland of Greece at the age of 12 to seek the ability to earn doweries such that his seven sisters could wed, he entered the New York harbor in 1911, unable to speak English and with a 7th grade education. Standing at the rail, which must have included a spraying of cold water as the waves crashed against the incoming ship, a new-found friend translated for him the words inscribed on the Statue of Liberty written by Emma Lazarus:

Give me your tired, your poor,
Your huddled masses yearning to breathe free,
The wretched refuse of your teeming shore.
Send these, the homeless, tempest-tossed, to me:
I lift my lamp beside the golden door.

Life was not easy. He started cleaning tables in a restaurant. His first purchases were a copy of the Constitution and a large history book on the U.S., which he read word-for-word in English. With each page turned as he painstakingly learned and read, his trust in his chosen government deepened. Twenty years later, he had paid doweries for six sisters, he owned his own restaurant in downtown Washington, D.C., married a young American of French ancestry who grew up in New Orleans, and adopted two abandoned children, one of whom is co-author of this book. Throughout his rich and giving life, even as his wealth and well-being waxed and waned, and as others continuously reached out to him for his wisdom and help, he trusted those welcoming words from the towering Lady in the harbor, he trusted his chosen government, he trusted the American dream.

Today, however, the landscape appears starkly different. That once-sturdy trust is being tested by the fragmentation of democracy. We find ourselves in a time marked by political polarization and extreme partisanship, where the very fabric of civil discourse is fraying. Misinformation spreads rapidly, eroding confidence in institutions that are meant to uphold democratic values. Social and economic disparities widen, contributing to a growing skepticism about whether these institutions truly serve the people or are beholden to other interests.

The change in the underlying values defining the American identity are complex and multifaceted, many reflecting broader social, political, and economic trends. Here are a few key aspects:

1. **Fear vs. Opportunity**. Historically, the United States has been seen as a land of opportunity for immigrants, a place where anyone could pursue their dreams and contribute to the nation's growth. In recent years, however, heightened fears over security and economic stability have led to restrictive immigration policies and attitudes, framing immigrants not as contributors but as potential threats.

2. **Individualism vs Community**. There has been a cultural shift toward greater individualism, sometimes at the expense of community and collective responsibility. This change can create divisions, as people prioritize personal success and security over communal well-being and support for others, including immigrants.

3. **Diversity vs Homogeneity**. The U.S. has long prided itself on being a melting pot, celebrating diversity as a strength. However, there's been increased tension around issues of race, ethnicity, gender, and sexual and cultural identity, with some factions pushing for a more homogeneous national identity, resistant to the cultural changes brought by the flow of global trade and immigration.

4. **Polarization and Misinformation.** Increasing political polarization has made constructive dialogue more challenging, and the spread of misinformation further complicates the ability to form a cohesive national narrative. These forces can contribute to misconceptions about diverse cultural groups and exacerbate divisions within society.

5. **Inclusion vs Exclusion.** There is an ongoing struggle between inclusive policies that aim to extend rights and opportunities to all people, regardless of background, and exclusionary policies that seek to limit access and maintain the status quo.

Addressing these shifts requires a conscious effort to foster understanding, empathy (the fundamental *strength* of Western Civilization), and a recommitment to the principles of equality that are foundational to the American identity. This moment can be an opportunity to redefine and strengthen democratic and societal values, ensuring they align more closely with principles of justice, equity, and transparency. It's a challenging yet pivotal time that could lead to meaningful transformation.

As we face these challenges, we must ask ourselves: *How did we arrive at this point of disillusionment?*

Fragmentation within a government can occur for various reasons, random firings and the dismantling of organizations points to some possible causes and effects of such fragmentation. Here are some aspects to consider:

1. **Leadership Changes and Turnover:** Frequent firings or resignations, particularly at high levels of government, can lead to instability and uncertainty within and between government agencies. This can hinder long-term planning and policy development. High turnover can result in a significant loss of institutional knowledge, as experienced personnel are replaced or leave. This can impact the effectiveness and efficiency of government operations.

2. **Policy Discontinuity:** With changes in leadership, there may be abrupt shifts in policy priorities, leading to inconsistent or fragmented policy implementation. This can be particularly disruptive in areas requiring sustained effort, such as social security, environmental regulation or healthcare. Fragmentation can cause delays in the implementation of existing policies or the creation of new ones, affecting overall governmental performance and public trust.

3. **Organizational Dismantling:** The dismantling of government agencies or programs can reduce the government's ability to address certain issues effectively, leading to gaps in service delivery or oversight. When organizations are abruptly dismantled, it erodes public confidence in government, as citizens may perceive these actions as undermining the stability and reliability of government functions.

4. **Impact on Stakeholders:** Other levels of government, private sector partners, and the public may experience confusion and disruption as continuity and coordination suffer. Fragmentation can have broader economic and social consequences, especially if affected organizations play critical roles in areas like public health, national security, or economic regulation.

5. **Checks and Balances:** Rapid or unchecked changes in the executive branch can challenge the effectiveness of legislative and judicial oversight, potentially leading to further fragmentation across branches of government.

When checks and balances are weakened or disregarded, and the executive branch operates with unchecked power, it can significantly contribute to governmental fragmentation through:

- *Decision-Making Bottlenecks.* With power concentrated in the executive, decision-making can become centralized and less inclusive. This can lead to fragmentation as other branches of government, like the legislative and judicial, may be sidelined, reducing their roles in shaping and overseeing policies.

- *Reduction in Accountability.* Without effective checks, there is less oversight of executive actions, which can lead to fragmented governance where accountability mechanisms are weak or absent.

- *Public Disillusionment.* When checks and balances are ignored, public trust in government institutions erode, leading to a fragmented society where citizens feel disconnected from centralized authority.

- *Polarization.* The absence of balanced governance can exacerbate political and social polarization, contributing to fragmentation along ideological lines.

- *Swinging Priorities.* Policies may become inconsistent, as the executive branch might rapidly change priorities without legislative collaboration or judicial oversight, leading to fragmented policy landscapes where initiatives lack cohesion.

- *State and Local Strain.* Subnational governments may feel fragmented from federal directives if state and local priorities clash with central executive decisions, leading to potential conflicts and inefficiencies.

- *Legislative and Judicial Marginalization.* When the executive branch overrides or bypasses the legislative and judicial branches, it weakens these institutions' ability to fulfill their roles, resulting in fragmented governance where institutional roles and responsibilities become blurred or ineffective.

- *Dismantling of Checks.* Continued exercise of power without restraint can lead to the dismantling of mechanisms designed to check executive actions, further entrenching fragmented and imbalanced governance.

- *Democratic Backsliding.* A lack of checks and balances can contribute to democratic backsliding, where democratic norms and institutions are eroded, leading to fragmented governance structures that struggle to effectively represent or respond to the citizenry.

- *Increased Corruption Risks.* Unchecked power increases the likelihood of corruption and abuse, fragmenting governmental integrity and transparency.

As can be seen, overall, maintaining robust checks and balances is crucial for preventing fragmentation, ensuring that governmental power is exercised in a balanced, accountable manner that upholds democratic principles and institutional integrity

Is it Possible to Rebuild Trust?

The relationship between trust and fragmentation is cyclical: fragmentation breeds distrust, and distrust further fragments democratic integrity. Rebuilding trust in fragmented democracies requires a multifaceted approach, requiring concerted efforts across multiple domains of society and governance by fostering openness, enhancing transparency, promoting dialogue across divides, and ensuring equitable representation in policy-making processes. Only by recognizing and validating each piece of this fragmented mosaic can democracies hope to restore trust and cohesion in their systems.

One key avenue for rebuilding trust is through institutional reform. Rothstein and Teorell argue that improving the quality of government, particularly in terms of impartiality and effectiveness, can significantly enhance public trust. As they state, "When government institutions are perceived as fair and competent, citizens are more likely to trust them and comply with their decisions." [*Reference:* Rothstein, B., & Teorell, J. (2008). What is quality of government? A theory of impartial government institutions. *Governance, 21*(2), 165-190, p. 170.]

Norris agrees, emphasizing the importance of institutional reform and increased civic engagement in addressing what she terms the "democratic deficit." This involves not only making institutions more transparent and accountable but also actively engaging citizens in the democratic process. Resilience in democratic systems can be enhanced by creating robust feedback mechanisms between government and citizens, fostering civic education, and promoting inclusive dialogue across different segments of society. Successful trust-rebuilding efforts often involve a combination of top-down institutional reforms and bottom-up civic initiatives. [*Reference:* Norris, P. (2011). *Democratic Deficit: Critical Citizens Revisited.* Cambridge University Press.]

Increasing opportunities for meaningful civic engagement help rebuild trust. Fung proposes that innovative forms of participatory governance can bridge the gap between citizens and institutions. He notes, "When citizens have real opportunities to shape public decisions, they develop greater trust in government and in each other". [*Reference:* Fung, A. (2015). Putting the public back into governance: The challenges of citizen participation and its future. Public Administration Review, 75(4), 513-522, p. 514.]

Addressing the spread of misinformation is crucial for rebuilding trust. Amazeen suggests that improving media literacy can help citizens navigate complex information environments. As she states, "Enhancing critical thinking skills and the ability to evaluate information sources can increase resistance to misinformation and rebuild trust in legitimate information sources". Clearly, critical thinking on the part of constituents is a necessity. [*Reference:* Amazeen, M. A. (2020). Journalistic interventions: The structural factors affecting the global emergence of fact-checking. *Journalism, 21*(1), 95-111, p. 1267.]

Rebuilding trust also requires addressing social fragmentation. Putnam argues that while diversity can initially reduce social trust, over time, societies can develop new forms of social solidarity. He suggests, "The central challenge for modern, diversifying societies is to create a new, broader sense of 'we'". [*Reference:* Putnam, R. D. (2007). E pluribus unum: Diversity and community in the twenty-first century. *Scandinavian Political Studies, 30*(2), 137-174, p. 139.]

The role of political leadership in rebuilding trust cannot be overstated. Hetherington and Rudolph argue that political leaders play a crucial role in shaping public trust. They note, "When political leaders demonstrate competence, integrity, and a commitment to the public good, they can significantly influence levels of public trust". [*Reference*: Hetherington, M. J., & Rudolph, T. J. (2015). Why Washington won't work: Polarization, political trust, and the governing crisis. University of Chicago Press, p. 34.]

In the digital age, rebuilding trust also involves leveraging technology effectively. Van Dijck and Alinejad suggest that digital platforms can be designed to foster trust and democratic engagement. As they argue, "By creating digital spaces that promote constructive dialogue and verified information, we can counteract some of the trust-eroding effects of social media". [*Reference:* Van Dijck, J., & Alinejad, D. (2020). Social media and trust in scientific expertise: Debating the Covid-19 pandemic. Social Media + Society, 6(4), 2056305120981057, p. 8.]

Finally, it's important to recognize that rebuilding trust is a long-term process. Norris emphasizes the need for sustained efforts, stating, "Rebuilding trust in democratic institutions requires consistent, long-term commitment to reform and engagement. Quick fixes are unlikely to produce lasting results." *Reference*: Norris, P. (2011). *Democratic Deficit: Critical citizens revisited.* Cambridge University Press, p. 242.

In Summary ...

While the task of rebuilding trust in fragmented democracies such as the United States is challenging, research across multiple disciplines suggests that it is possible. It requires a multifaceted approach involving institutional reform, increased civic engagement, media literacy, efforts to bridge social divides, responsible leadership, effective use of technology, and a long-term commitment to these goals. By addressing these various aspects simultaneously, democracies can work towards restoring the trust that is fundamental to their functioning and legitimacy.

As public trust erodes, the collective demand for transparency, accountability, and truth becomes even more pronounced. Many citizens become more vigilant and critical of the narratives and policies put forth by those in power. This breaking point can serve as a catalyst for change, where the pressure to address systemic issues becomes unavoidable. The key is to channel this critical awareness into positive action. **Only first, at least for the U.S., the American people must choose to do so.**

Chapter 11
Sowing Fragmentation

Societal political fragmentation can be seen as both a tool and a byproduct of power dynamics in various governance structures. In this setting, fragmentation can arise either intentionally, as a strategic choice, or unintentionally, as an inadvertent consequence of actions or policies. Intentional fragmentation is often employed as a technique to consolidate authority by disrupting cohesion within the community, making it harder for unified opposition to form. Similarly, an established order might unintentionally sow fragmentation through incidental decisions that accentuate societal divisions. Understanding the implications of both intentional and unintentional fragmentation allows us to better navigate and counter these dynamics in real-world scenarios.

In today's rapidly evolving political landscape, it's crucial to explore how these dynamics can play out within a regime—be it fictional or real. Fragmentation is not simply the absence of order or unity; it can be a deliberate, tactical maneuver by those in power to maintain their dominance. To understand this concept more thoroughly, let's delve into a fictional example that illustrates how fragmentation might serve an autocratic government in achieving its objectives while managing societal divisions to sustain power.

A Fictional Example

Fragmentation can prove advantageous for an autocratic form of government. Building on the types of societal fragmentation, let's see how fragmentation might serve a small autocratic regime, leveraging societal fragmentation to consolidate power.

1. **Divide and Rule**. By fragmenting society, an autocratic government can weaken organized opposition. Divided groups find it harder to unite against the government, thus prolonging the regime's hold on power. *Detail:* Autocratic regimes can exploit societal divisions to prevent the formation of unified opposition movements. By keeping various social, ethnic, or ideological groups at odds, the regime reduces the chance of a cohesive resistance forming. [*Reference:* Paxton, R. O. (2005). *The Anatomy of Fascism.* Vintage.]

Example: In the fictional country of Zaternik, the Autarch's regime faced increasing discontent among its ethnically diverse population. The regime quietly fueled longstanding rivalries between the northern Tribali and southern Akkari peoples by supporting cultural events that highlighted their differences and rewriting school texts to emphasize historical conflicts. As the tension escalated into sporadic skirmishes, the Autarch stepped in as a mediator, presenting his leadership as the only solution capable of averting a full-scale conflict. With opposition movements unable to unite across ethnic lines, the regime's control remained unchallenged.

2. **Control Over Information**. By fostering division, the regime can create conflicting accounts, making it difficult for citizens to discern the truth. *Detail:* Fragmentation allows governments to manipulate information streams. By controlling the narrative and fostering conflicting accounts, it becomes difficult for citizens to identify unbiased truth, thus securing the regime's image. *Reference:* George Orwell's *1984* . Though fictional, this novel explores themes of propaganda and information control in a totalitarian state.

Example: Zaternik's government owned the major media outlets and fed the public conflicting narratives about the economic downturn. Competing news channels broadcast partisan analyses, each blaming a different minority for the nation's woes. While one channel pointed fingers at foreign migrants, another scapegoated internal dissidents. Citizens, bombarded by a confusing array of "truths," struggled to discern reality from propaganda. The resulting ambiguity upheld the Autarch's cultivated image as the only stalwart against chaos, securing his grip on power amid the turmoil.

3. **Maintaining Political Stability.** Social fragmentation can lead to a lack of collective action by dispersing public grievances across different sectors of society, each with its unique issues and demands. *Detail:* By spreading public grievances across various groups, a fragmented society finds it harder to rally collectively against the governing regime, thus stabilizing the autocracy by reducing large-scale dissent. [*Reference:* Sunstein, Cass R. *Going to Extremes: How Like Minds Unite and Divide*. Discusses how division can prevent unified action, relevant to understanding collective action dynamics.]

Example: Confronting the rise of a charismatic opposition leader, the Autarch devised a strategy to maintain stability by permitting grievances to fester without coalescing. Zaternik's government created multiple small social programs, each targeting only a specific interest group—farmers, urban workers, young professionals—ensuring that each received just enough attention to prevent collective mobilization. This fragmented approach kept each constituency focused on narrow concerns, diluting the potential for unified dissent.

4. **Exploiting Differences.** The government can exploit societal divisions to pit groups against each other, thus diverting attention from its own governance shortcomings and maintaining power through distraction. *Detail:* The government might intentionally pit different societal groups against one another, using state resources or policies to favor certain groups, which maintains power through distraction from its governance issues. [*Reference:* Divide and Rule tactics are explored historically in *Colonialism in Question: Theory, Knowledge, History* by Frederick Cooper. It provides examples of using societal divisions for control.]

Example: In Zaternik, the Autarch capitalized on the provincial rivalry between coastal and inland regions. By promising increased infrastructure spending in the coastal cities, he spurred jealousy among inland leaders, compelling them to vie for similar attention. The government further stoked division by inviting local inland chiefs to participate in national councils, seemingly empowering them while actually entangling them in bureaucratic procedures that yielded little actual influence. These moves occupied regional leaders with infighting, allowing the Autarch to deflect criticism from his central administration.

5. **Legitimizing Authority.** By framing itself as the only entity capable of managing a fragmented and chaotic societal structure, the regime can justify authoritarian measures and policies. *Detail:* By creating or emphasizing societal chaos, the regime can position itself as the necessary stabilizing force, legitimizing authoritarian policies and governance as means to restore order. [*Reference:* Alexis de Tocqueville's *Democracy in America* examines how perceived threats can be used to justify concentrations of power.]

Example: After orchestrating a calculated release of conflicting reports on potential threats from neighboring countries, the Autarch seized the opportunity to declare a state of emergency. Military parades and public safety campaigns were launched, casting the regime as the vigilant protector of Zaternik against invented external dangers. The heightened tension justified the deployment of authoritarian measures, such as curfews and surveillance, with citizens largely accepting these intrusions as necessary for national safety.

6. **Economic Advantage.** Fragmentation might allow an autocratic government to control economic resources more effectively by allocating them selectively to maintain loyalty among certain groups. *Detail:* An autocratic government might selectively distribute economic resources to maintain loyalty among certain fragmented groups, converting economic leverage into political capital. [*Reference: The Political Economy of Dictatorship* by Ronald Wintrobe provides insights into how dictators use economic means for political ends].

Example: Striving for loyalty among the Zaternik elite, the Autarch selectively awarded lucrative contracts and development projects to supporters in key business sectors. This preferential treatment entrenched economic dependency among these elites, ensuring their allegiance. Meanwhile, the broader population saw uneven development and unequal access to opportunities, intensifying social divisions but binding powerful economic partners closer to the regime.

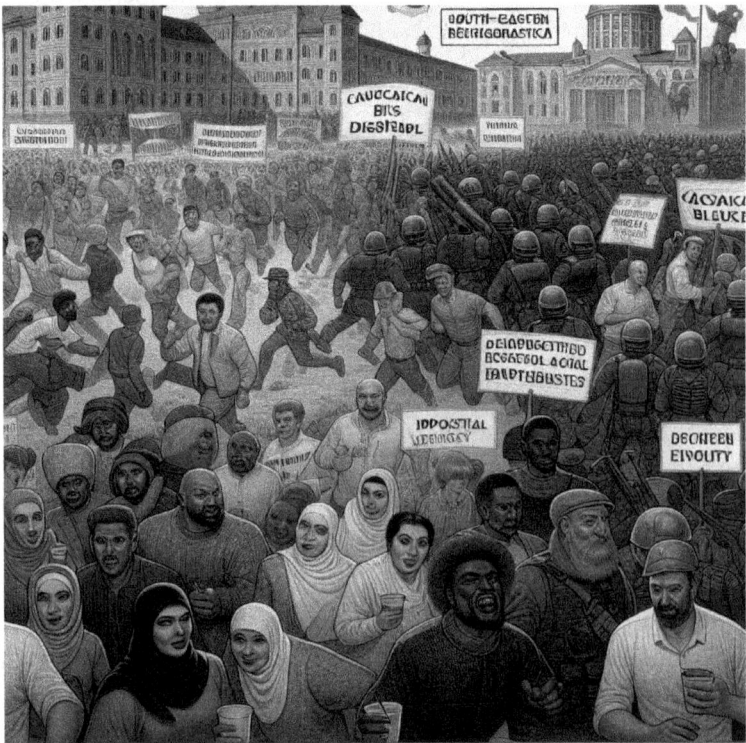

Societal Fragmentation in Zaternik

Through these intertwined talks, Zaternik's autocratic government exemplifies how societal fragmentation can be strategically manipulated to sustain power and control, often at the expense of unity and long-term stability and causing both short and long-term harms to portions of the populace. The immediate question that comes to mind is: *How can people push against this?* Once recognized, *How can an individual try to improve this situation?*

The Zaternik People's Response

Pushing against societal fragmentation under an autocratic regime can be challenging, but individuals and communities can take several meaningful actions to improve the situation. In Zaternik a group of ethnically-diverse leaders began to emerge, urged forward by worsening conditions and recognizing that there was more opportunity for improvement in working together. Let's explore the "meaningful actions" that this group and the open-minded citizens of Zaternik decided to take.

1. **Promote Dialogue and Understanding**. *Facilitate Conversations:* Encourage open, respectful discussions among diverse groups to foster mutual understanding and dispel misconceptions. Creating safe spaces for dialogue can help bridge divides. *Community Engagement:* Participate in or organize community events that celebrate diversity and unity, promoting cross-cultural friendships and collaborations.

2. **Educate and Empower.** *Spread Awareness:* Educate yourself and others about the tactics used by autocratic regimes to promote division. Sharing this knowledge can empower communities to resist manipulation. *Advocate for Critical Thinking:* Encourage critical analysis of media and official narratives to combat misinformation. Supporting educational initiatives that promote independent thought is crucial.

3. **Strengthen Civil Society.** *Support Local Organizations:* Back NGOs and community groups focused on human rights, social justice, and inclusive policies. These organizations play a vital role in advocating for reforms and providing support. *Volunteer and Collaborate:* Back NGOs and community groups focused on human rights, social justice, and inclusive policies. These organizations play a vital role in advocating for reforms and providing support.

4. **Leverage Technology.** *Utilize Social Media Wisely:* Use social media platforms to share factual information and build networks of support. Online communities can unite individuals across geographical and social boundaries. *Digital Literacy:* Promote digital literacy to help others recognize bias and misinformation online.

5. **Active Participation in Governance:** *Engage in Civic Processes:* Exercise your right to vote and participate in local governance, even in challenging environments. Civic engagement is essential for voicing collective concerns and influencing policy. *Advocate for Fair Policies:* Campaign for policies that promote equality, transparency, and accountability, building momentum for systemic change.

6. **Build Global Alliances.** *Connect Internationally:* Campaign for policies that promote equality, transparency, and accountability, building momentum for systemic change.

These steps certainly contribute to building a more cohesive, informed, and resilient society, helping to counteract the fragmentation and divisive strategies employed by autocratic regimes. For Zaternik, it appears the journey home has started, and as the next election comes closer, we can imagine a shift in political power, a shift that will reengage the will of the people.

Targeting Education

Throughout history, education has frequently been targeted by those seeking greater wealth and power, as controlling or limiting knowledge can be a powerful means of maintaining authority. Here are a few reasons why education is often attacked by such individuals.

1. **Maintaining Control.** By restricting access to education, those in power can limit critical thinking and dissent. An educated populace is more likely to question authority and demand accountability, posing a threat to those who wish to maintain control. An example is the Taliban's ban on girls' education (Afghanistan, 1996-2001; 2021-present). The Taliban's rule included a ban on girls attending school beyond a certain age, severely restricting educational access for women and girls. This attack on education was aimed at maintaining traditional gender roles and control over the population. A second example is the cultural revolution in China (1966-1976). Under Mao Zedong, the Chinese government sought to eliminate "bourgeois" elements from Chinese society, which led to the closure of schools and universities. Intellectuals were persecuted, and "Red Guards" were encouraged to attack cultural and educational institutions. This period severely disrupted education and contributed to a loss of educational and intellectual capital in China.

2. **Preserving Hierarchies.** Education can be a great equalizer, providing opportunities for social mobility and empowerment. Those in entrenched positions of power may fear losing their dominance if more people gain the skills and knowledge to challenge existing hierarchies. An example is

Apartheid in South Africa (1948-1994). During Apartheid, the South African government implemented the Bantu Education Act, which created an education system designed to limit the economic potential and personal growth of Black South Africans. This severely restricted educational opportunities and reinforced systemic inequality.

3. **Limiting Information.** Education often brings a broader understanding of the world, including awareness of rights, freedoms, and injustices, understanding what is possible. By controlling educational content or access, powerful individuals can shape narratives and maintain a preferred status quo. An example is the cuts to arts education in the United States (1980s and 1990s). In various states in the U.S., education budgets were reduced, leading to significant cuts in arts education. In addition to suppressing free creative thought, this was partly due to a shift toward emphasizing subjects believed to directly correlate with economic growth, such as math and science, at the expense of holistic educational experiences.

4. **Suppressing Innovation.** With education comes innovation and change, which can disrupt established economic and political systems. Those who benefit from the current systems may attack educational initiatives that promote new ideas that could threaten their interests. An example of suppressing innovation can be drawn from the Soviet Union during the later years of its existence. The Soviet government heavily controlled and directed scientific research and technological development, focusing efforts on projects that aligned with its ideological and political priorities, such as military and space advancements. This focus often came at the expense of other scientific fields and technological innovations that could challenge centralized authority or the planned economy. For instance, while Soviet leaders ambitiously pursued spacecraft and nuclear armament advancements, other areas such as computing technology lagged significantly behind Western countries. This deliberate control over the types of innovation encouraged and permitted resulted in technological stagnation in many sectors, as explorations of potentially disruptive innovations were suppressed to maintain the political and economic status quo.

5. **Cultural Manipulation.** Education can promote cultural exchange and understanding, but autocrats might prefer to promote a singular cultural or ideological narrative. By controlling education, they can reinforce this narrative and suppress diverse viewpoints. An example is the book burnings in Nazi Germany (1933). The Nazi regime conducted book burnings to destroy works that were considered "un-German." This was

part of a broader effort to control education and suppress intellectual dissent, aligning educational content strictly with Nazi ideology. A second example is the control over education in Eastern Bloc Countries during the Cold War Era. In several Eastern Bloc countries during the Cold War, education was tightly controlled to align with communist ideology. Curricula were adjusted to prevent the spread of Western ideas, while access to higher education was often limited to those loyal to the regime.

As history has shown, targeting education is a common tactic used by those in power to maintain control, preserve hierarchical structures, limit information, suppress innovation, and manipulate cultural narratives. These actions reflect a broader pattern of undermining societal pillars that foster equality, critical thinking, and progress. This sets the stage for examining how similar strategies of division and control are being employed domestically. Transitioning our focus to the contemporary landscape, the current fragmentation within the U.S. government is revealing itself not merely as a byproduct of political shifts but as a deliberate strategy by those seeking to reshape societal norms. By purportedly aiming for efficiency, efforts are underway to dismantle or weaken the very structures that promote social cohesion and unify diverse communities. Let's dig deeper.

Sowing Fragmentation in the U.S.

The fragmentation occurring in the U.S. government is intentional and purposeful, that is, happening through the choices made by an increasingly autocratic government to intentionally fragment society. The approach is—in the name of efficiency—to undermine and/or dismantle the structures and practices that traditionally promote social cohesion and unity.

Building on the understanding gained from our earlier discussion of political fragmentation and our fictional example of Zaternik, the specific strategy to fragment the U.S. government, now in full swing, can be, at least partially, framed as:

1. **Encourage Political Polarization**. *Exploit Divisions:* Amplify political divides through rhetoric or policy choices that pit groups against each other. *Undermine Political Dialogue:* Disrupt forums and processes designed for bipartisan or multiparty dialogue to prevent consensus-building and increase fragmentation.

2. **Exacerbate Economic Inequality.** *Unequal Resource Distribution*: Implement policies that widen the gap between wealthy and poorer citizens create further economic divisions, leading to social unrest. *Reduce Support for Social Safety Nets:* Withdraw support from programs that level

the playing field, such as education and healthcare, to deepen social divides.

3. **Weaken Institutions**. *Destabilize Public Institutions:* Erode trust in key institutions like the judiciary or media to increase social fragmentation by reducing their effectiveness and perceived legitimacy. *Restrict Civil Participation:* Limit opportunities for civic engagement and dismantle platforms for community involvement such as theatres and art institutions to establish greater societal disconnection.

4. **Restrict Education and Civic Engagement.** *Control Education Content:* Manipulate educational content to diminish critical thinking. Promote biased narratives to fragment intellectual unity and understanding. Encourage "book banning and burning" to shift current and historical thinking along the lines of the desired narrative. *Reduce Civic Education:* Limit systems that teach the importance of civic responsibility and democratic participation to weaken community bonds.

5. **Promote Exclusive Narratives.** *Initiate Continuous Divisive Media Campaigns:* Use media to propagate divisive narratives and misinformation in order to deepen societal divides and create echo chambers.

6. **Undermine Inclusivity and Diversity.** *Promote Homogeneity:* Policies or campaigns that suppress cultural, religious, gender, sexual or ethnic diversity marginalize minority groups and erode societal cohesion. *Discourage Multicultural Initiatives:* Reduce support for multiculturalism and diversity initiatives to limit opportunities for different groups to engage positively.

The important concept being attacked through undermining inclusivity and diversity demands a deeper look. *When a government is intentionally aimed toward fragmenting society, targeting inclusivity and diversity is a strategic focus.* Inclusivity and diversity are foundational to social cohesion, as they promote understanding and cooperation among different groups. Undermining these aspects exacerbates societal divisions. By targeting inclusivity and diversity, the U.S. government is systematically eroding the very mechanisms that help build a cohesive and harmonious society, resulting in increased fragmentation and societal discord.

Let's break that down even further by exploring specifically how targeting inclusivity and diversity contributes to fragmentation. First, *through discrimination and exclusion,* which marginalizes minority groups. Implementing policies or practices that discriminate against or exclude minority groups can create divisions, fostering resentment and social tension. Second, *through reducing support for multicultural initiatives*. Restricting platforms that support multicultural expression and interaction leads to cultural isolation and prevents the integration of diverse perspectives.

Third, *by promoting uniformity*. Encouraging uniformity over diversity can marginalize those who don't conform to the majority, leading to feelings of alienation and division. Fourth, *by undermining anti-discrimination efforts*. Weakening protections by reducing legal and institutional protections against discrimination increases instances of bias and inequality, deepening societal fractures. And fifth, *by controlling the narrative*. Propagating exclusive ideologies through promoting narratives that favor a specific group alienates others, fostering the "us-versus-them" mentality.

In Summary ...

With our deeper understanding of the causes behind societal political fragmentation, we can strategically address its challenges by employing the Knowledge Capacity of Reversal. This approach allows us to take what initially appears as a destabilizing force and transform it into an opportunity for positive change and growth. By recognizing the deliberate and incidental factors contributing to fragmentation, we can move toward effectively counteracting its negative impacts. This involves fostering unity and dialogue, promoting inclusivity, and reinforcing democratic principles to rebuild cohesion within our communities. Embracing this proactive mindset enables us to cultivate a more resilient and harmonious society, turning fragmentation from a divisive force into a catalyst for constructive improvement and collaboration.

Chapter 12
Seeking AI-Infused Cohesion

As we move into an unprecedented future, we recognize that Artificial Intelligence has the capacity to both help reduce and increase fragmentation in every area of our lives. Let's explore a few examples. Here are some of the ways AI offers the potential to help reduce fragmentation.

- *Enhanced Communication and Understanding.* AI can facilitate better communication across cultural and linguistic barriers, bringing people closer. Translation tools and AI-driven platforms can promote global dialogue and understanding.

- *Data-Driven Solutions.* AI can analyze complex data to offer insights and solutions to global challenges, such as climate change, by helping coordinate international efforts and creating unified responses.

- *Increasing Accessibility.* AI can enhance access to education and healthcare, bridging gaps in underserved communities, reducing inequalities, and promoting social cohesion.

- *Personalized Learning and Growth.* AI systems can offer personalized content that promotes understanding and empathy, helping individuals grow beyond their biases and encouraging cohesive communities.

Conversely, here are some ways providing the potential for AI to increase fragmentation:

- *Echo Chambers and Polarization.* Algorithms designed for personalization can create echo chambers by showing users content that reinforces their beliefs, potentially increasing polarization.

- *Job Displacement.* As AI systems automate tasks, economic inequality could widen if new policies and education systems are not implemented to support displaced workers, leading to further societal fragmentation.

- *Bias and Inequality.* If not carefully managed, AI systems can perpetuate or amplify biases present in their training data, leading to unfair treatment and deepening existing societal divisions.

- *Surveillance and Privacy Issues.* The use of AI for surveillance can lead to trust issues and divisions between governments and citizens, as well as among states, depending on how it's used geopolitically.

As can be seen from this quick synthesis, ultimately, the impact of AI on fragmentation will depend significantly on human choices around its ethical development and implementation. Responsible AI governance, along with inclusive and transparent policymaking, will play critical roles in ensuring technology helps unify rather than divide.

The integration of AI, including generative AI, influences digital fragmentation and a country's global power dynamics in various ways. Countries leading in AI research and development can set technological standards and attract global investments, increasing their influence. Leadership in AI can attract talent and boost *economic growth*, enhancing a nation's global standing. Nations developing robust AI ecosystems, including data infrastructure, talent pipelines, and supportive policies, can become hubs of innovation. This, as we know, can lead to technological fragmentation where AI capabilities differ significantly across regions.

Countries with strong AI *regulations and ethical frameworks* can influence global AI policies. By setting high standards, they can lead international discourse and encourage other nations to adopt similar regulations. Diverse approaches to AI regulation can lead to fragmented digital environments [digital regulatory fragmentation], where companies must navigate differing rules and standards in various countries.

AI's ability to automate processes and enhance *decision-making* can drive economic growth, giving technologically advanced nations a competitive advantage. As AI reshapes industries, countries must adapt or risk economic fragment. Those unable to integrate AI technologies effectively may fall behind.

In *security and defense*, AI can improve cybersecurity strategies, allowing nations to better protect digital infrastructure and maintain control. Military applications of AI can shift power dynamics, with countries investing in AI-enhanced defense systems potentially gaining strategic advantages.

Finally, let's address *social and ethical considerations*. Generative AI can create content that shapes cultural narratives and public opinion, influencing global culture and information flow. However, the ethical dilemmas surrounding AI usage, such as bias or privacy concerns, can lead to social fragmentation if not addressed consistently worldwide.

Exacerbating and Mitigating

As can be seen by this quick introduction, AI has the potential to either exacerbate or mitigate digital fragmentation, depending on how countries leverage technology, regulate its use, and collaborate internationally. Successful navigation of these factors can enhance a country's global influence, while failure to do so can result in increasing isolation or dependency.

Here's a conceptual chart contrasting the use of AI to exacerbate or mitigate digital fragmentation.

Aspect	AI Use to Exacerbate Fragmentation	AI Use to Mitigate Fragmentation
Economic Impact	Automation leading to job displacement, increasing economic inequality and fragmentation.	AI-driven economic growth can create new job opportunities and enhance equality bridging economic divides.
Technological Leadership	Nations with advanced AI may dominate technology, creating a tech gap and regional fragmentation.	Collaborative AI advancements can be shared internationally promoting global tech convergence.
Regulatory Environment	Diverse AI regulations can lead to incompatible systems across borders.	Standardized globally coordinated regulations can unify AI systems and reduce fragmentation
Dada Privacy and Security	Surveillance AI can increase state control, fragmenting individual freedoms.	AI can enhance data protection tools, fostering trust and reducing privacy concerns across regions.
Cultural Influence	Generative AI can produce biased content, polarizing societies.	AI can promote cultural exchange and understanding by translating and disseminating diverse content.
Social Inequality	AI tools may only be accessible to wealthier nations or demographics, deepening divides.	AI can be used to provide educational tools and resources to underserved areas, narrowing inequality gaps.
Global Collaboration	AI-driven competition might prioritize national interests over global welfare, leading to geopolitical fragmentation.	AI can facilitate international research collaboration, solving global issues such as climate change collectively.

This chart illustrates the dual nature of AI in relation to digital fragmentation, again, emphasizing that its impact largely depends on how it's implemented and managed globally. A country aspiring to lead the world in AI while also seeking to control faces a complex balancing act. Let's explore how these aims can both align and conflict.

Compatible Aspects

1. **Setting Standards**: *Regulatory Leadership.* By establishing robust ethical and regulatory frameworks for AI, a country can set global standards that others might follow, thereby exerting influence and control over how AI evolves worldwide.

2. **Driving Innovation:** *Investment in R&D.* Leading in AI requires significant investment in research and development. By fostering innovation, a country can maintain control over cutting-edge technologies and direct their applications.

3. **Talent Development and Retention:** *Educational Initiatives.* Building a skilled workforce through targeted education and training in AI can help a country dominate AI advancements while maintaining control over development processes.

4. **Infrastructure Development:** *Building AI Ecosystems.* Developing AI infrastructure can enable a country to be at the forefront of AI innovation, providing the tools and environments needed to lead on a global scale.

Conflicting Aspects:

1. **Openness versus Control:** *Global Collaboration.* Leading in AI often requires international cooperation and data sharing, which can be at odds with tight control over information and technology.

2. **Ethical Concerns:** *Bias and Privacy Issues.* Over-control in AI deployment might lead to ethical issues, such as biased algorithms or surveillance concerns, which can damage a country's global leadership reputation.

3. **Innovation Stifling:** *Limiting Creativity.* Too much control can stifle innovation by limiting the free exploration and experimentation that drive AI advancements.

4. **Geopolitical Tensions:** *International Regulations.* Efforts to control AI domestically might clash with international norms and regulations, potentially leading to geopolitical tensions.

In essence, while it's possible for a country to both lead and control AI, achieving this requires careful policy design that promotes innovation and collaboration while ensuring ethical standards and security are maintained. Balancing these components is critical to reconciling leadership with control.

The difficulty comes into play when there are no ethical standards governing the development and use of AI. Potential negative consequences include:

(1) *Bias and discrimination* through unchecked algorithms. Without ethical oversight, AI systems might perpetuate or even exacerbate existing biases, leading to discriminatory outcomes in areas like hiring, law enforcement, and lending.

(2) *Privacy violations* through data misuse. The lack of ethical standards can result in the misuse of personal data, with AI systems collecting and analyzing information without consent, potentially violating privacy rights.

(3) *Lack of accountability* concerning blame and responsibility. Without ethical guidelines, it can be difficult to determine who is responsible for AI decisions, particularly those leading to harm or unfairness, leaving affected individuals without recourse.

(4) *Surveillance and control* through government overreach. AI systems could be used for mass surveillance or to infringe on civil liberties if ethical standards do not restrict these applications to protect individual freedoms.

(5) *Unfair competitive advantage* through market manipulation. Companies might exploit AI to gain unfair advantages, such as price manipulation or spreading misinformation, negatively impacting market integrity and consumer trust.

(6) *Safety concerns* with risky deployments. AI systems might be deployed without adequate testing or consideration of safety implications, leading to accidents or harm, especially in critical areas like healthcare or autonomous vehicles.

(7) *Erosion of trust* with loss of public confidence. The absence of ethical standards can erode public trust in AI technologies, resulting in resistance to their adoption and limiting potential benefits.

As can be seen, without ethical standards AI systems may produce unfair, biased or harmful outcomes, leading to public distrust. If people perceive AI as a threat to their rights or well-being, they may resist its adoption, stalling technological advancement and innovation. Therefore, to harness AI's full potential, it is essential to integrate ethical standards into its development and deployment, ensuring that AI technologies are fair, transparent, accountable, and beneficial to society as a whole, which are exactly the attributes of good government.

[DALL-E Contribution]
AI-Infused Cohesion: Learning from the Natural World

Connecting Human Values and AI

As we delve deeper into the potential of Artificial Intelligence (AI) to shape our global future, it becomes increasingly vital to recognize that technology must not only serve functional purposes but also embody the values that define us as human beings. Just as the human heart is central to life, metaphorically representing empathy, intuition, and compassion, so too must AI systems be guided by principles that mirror these qualities. In the intersection of human values and technological advancement lies the key to crafting AI that is trusted and embraced by society.

Thus, while AI excels in processing vast amounts of data, making precise decisions, and recognizing complex patterns, its impact hinges on its ability to align with human-centric values. The integration of empathy, creativity, and communication within AI systems contributes to their acceptance, effectiveness, and long-term success. This connection leads to technology that reflects societal norms and respects cultural and ethical diversity.

By instilling these "heart-like" qualities into AI, we craft systems that do not merely perform tasks but also build trust and cooperation, addressing various dimensions of digital fragmentation. AI's potential to learn, adapt, and make decisions in ways that relate to human intuition and empathy facilitates more supportive interactions. This alignment with human values creates an environment where AI is not just seen as a tool but as a partner in addressing complex global challenges.

The human qualities that we suggest are empathy, intuition, compassion, creativity, decision-making, learning from experience, and communication. These qualities play crucial roles in bridging gaps in a fragmented world. *Empathy* helps individuals and communities understand and appreciate different perspectives. In a world often divided by cultural, political, and social differences, empathy fosters connections by enabling people to feel and understand the experiences of others, potentially reducing tensions and promoting unity.

Intuition can guide individuals and leaders in making decisions that consider unforeseen or intangible factors. In complex global issues where not all variables are known, intuition allows people to make more holistic decisions that might integrate various fragmented pieces of information. *Compassion* drives efforts to alleviate suffering and address inequalities. In a fragmented world, compassion can lead to actions and policies that address disparities, bringing communities together through shared efforts to improve living conditions and promote social justice.

Creativity is essential for developing innovative solutions to complex problems that contribute to world fragmentation. It encourages thinking outside conventional frameworks, fostering collaboration across different disciplines and cultures to craft unified approaches to global challenges. *Effective decision-making* helps navigate diverse and sometimes conflicting interests in a fractured world. By integrating logical reasoning with ethical considerations, individuals and organizations can make decisions that promote harmony and collective well-being.

Learning from past experiences enables societies to avoid repeating mistakes and to build on successful initiatives. This capacity is crucial in a fragmented world where understanding historical and cultural contexts can help bridge divides and foster reconciliation. *Open and effective communication* is key to resolving conflicts and sharing ideas. It helps in breaking down barriers and building bridges between disparate groups, promoting understanding and collaboration in a world where misinformation and miscommunication often contribute to division.

These heart-driven elements are essential in addressing and potentially healing the fragmentation seen in today's world. They highlight the importance of emotional intelligence, ethical reasoning, and collaborative efforts in fostering a more connected and cohesive global society. Here's a detailed comparison of each human element alongside its AI equivalent, with a focus on the human perspective.

Human Element (Heart)	Description from Human Perspective	AI Equivalent	Description
Empathy	Empathy involves the ability to understand and share the feelings of another person. It is an emotional connection that enables individuals to respond with care and compassion.	Sentiment Analysis	AI can analyze text or speech to identify emotional tones and respond based on predefined frameworks although it lacks true emotional comprehension.
Intuition	Intuition is a non-linear form of understanding where individuals draw on past experiences and knowledge to make judgments or solve problems without explicit reasoning.	Pattern Recognition	AI detects patterns in data using algorithms to predict or classify information, akin to intuitive guessing but based on vast computational analysis.
Compassion	Compassion involves recognizing suffering in others and feeling motivated to alleviate it. It is deeply connected to empathy and requires emotional engagement.	Adaptive Algorithms	AI can be designed to provide resources or actions that mimic compassionate gestures, but this is purely functional without any emotional involvement.
Creativity	Human creativity is the ability to generate novel and original ideas, often influenced by emotions, experiences, and cultural context. It involves imagination and personal expression.	Generative Models	AI uses computational methods to create new content (art, music, writing) derived from patterns and data it has processed, lacking originality and emotional depth.
Decision-Making	Human decision-making is a complex process that involves intuition, reasoning, emotions, and values. Decisions are often influenced by personal and social contexts.	Decision tree & Neural Networks	AI systems evaluate data through structured algorithms to make decisions with logical precision, devoid of emotional or ethical considerations.
Learning from Experience	Humans learn through experiences, reflection, and interaction. Learning is influenced by emotions, social contexts, and individual motivations.	Machine Learning	AI learns by adjusting algorithms based on data inputs reining models through feedback loops, similar to experiential learning, but without consciousness or personal growth.
Communication	Human communication is nuanced, involving language, tone, body, and context. It is	Natural Language Processing	AI processes and generates human language to facilitate communication, focusing on

	deeply tied to emotions and social connections.		syntactic and semantic structures rather than genuine understanding or emotional context.

This comparison highlights the depth and complexity inherent in human experiences and emotions, contrasting them with the computational and mechanical nature of AI systems. While AI can mimic certain functions of the human "heart" in a technical sense, it lacks the authentic emotional and conscious experiences that define human interactions. As illustrated in the table, the parallels between the human heart and AI functions emphasize the capacity for technology to reflect human values, enhancing both its acceptance and reliability. However, for AI to truly serve its purpose in fostering cohesion and bridging divides, it must be anchored in trust.

The integration of attributes such as empathy through sentiment analysis and creativity via generative models speaks to AI's evolving ability to connect with human experiences. Yet, trust is the cornerstone that ensures these capabilities are harnessed ethically and effectively. A society's willingness to embrace AI technologies, particularly those influencing critical sectors such as healthcare, education, and governance, depends on the assurance that—just is as expected of the government—AI operates with *integrity and respect for individual rights.*

Looking from the broader context of AI and trust, the quest to ensure that AI resonates with human values serves as a foundation for building cohesive technological and social systems. When we harmonize the technical prowess of AI with the deeply ingrained principles of empathy, compassion, and ethical integrity, we strengthen the trust necessary for global AI systems to thrive. This interplay of human and machine attributes positions AI as a unifying force capable of bridging divides and fostering a more connected, harmonious world.

Fragmentation and Trust in AI

Fragmentation plays a significant role in the discussion of trust and global leadership in AI in several ways. First, in *standardization challenges.* Fragmentation in AI development can lead to inconsistent standards and practices across different countries or organizations. This inconsistency makes it challenging to create universal benchmarks, complicating efforts to establish trust. Second, in *regulatory complexity.* Variations in AI regulations across different jurisdictions can create a fragmented landscape where companies must navigate complex and sometimes conflicting legal requirements. This regulatory fragmentation can hinder global cooperation and the seamless integration of AI technologies. Third, in *technology disparities.* Fragmentation can result in unequal access to AI technologies, with some regions advancing rapidly while others lag behind. This disparity can exacerbate global inequalities and potentially foster mistrust between nations, as those left behind may feel disadvantaged.

Fourth, in *cultural and ethical differences*. Fragmentation in cultural and ethical perspectives can lead to different expectations and trust levels in AI systems. AI applications that are accepted in one cultural context might face resistance in another, highlighting the need for culturally sensitive approaches. Fifth, in *data access and privacy*. Differences in data privacy laws and data access restrictions can lead to fragmented data environments. This fragmentation complicates the development of AI systems that rely on diverse and comprehensive datasets, possibly limiting AI's effectiveness and trustworthiness. And sixth, in *geopolitical tensions*. Geopolitical fragmentation can lead to differing AI strategies, with countries pursuing competing interests. This competition can hinder collaboration, increase suspicion, and reduce the potential for collective advancements in AI.

Addressing fragmentation must occur in AI development to foster trust. This involves harmonizing standards, encouraging cross-border cooperation, and building inclusive frameworks that respect cultural and ethical diversity. By doing so, the global AI community can work towards a cohesive and trusted technological landscape. The table below illustrates how fragmentation in various aspects of AI development can influence trust, emphasizing that overcoming fragmentation is vital for building and maintaining trust in AI technologies.

Aspect	Fragmentation Effect	Impact on Trust
Standardization	Fragmentation leads to inconsistent standards globally.	Trust is reduced as stakeholders lack common benchmarks for AI systems.
Regulatory Environment	Varying regulations create a complex legal landscape.	Trust in AI's compliance and safety is diminished, complicating international cooperation.
Technological Access	Technological disparities create uneven development.	Trust is eroded as regions perceiving themselves disadvantaged may distrust AI motives.
Cultural and Ethical Norms	Diverse ethical perspectives cause ethical fragmentation.	Trust varies, depending on how well AI aligns with local cultural values.
Data Availability	Differences in data laws lead to isolated data environments.	Trust in AI's effectiveness is compromised due to limited data.

Geopolitical Dynamics	Competing national interests foster geopolitical divides.	Trust declines as countries become wary of AI's use as a strategic tool.
Interoperability	Fragmentation causes systems to be non-interoperable.	Lack of seamless interaction diminishes trust in the technology's utility and reliability.

As we end our exploration into the intricacies of how AI can influence digital fragmentation and impact global power dynamics, it's crucial to underscore the potential of AI to foster not just division, but unity. In a world increasingly defined by technological complexity, AI has emerged as a double-edged sword—one capable of both deepening divides and bridging gaps. By strategically leveraging AI, nations can transform the prospects of fragmented societies, becoming beacons of cohesion rather than contributors to discord.

As has surfaced, the path towards AI-infused cohesion involves embracing ethical standards, fostering collaboration, and ensuring inclusivity. By setting high ethical benchmarks, countries can guide AI development towards outcomes that are fair, transparent, and accountable. These standards help mitigate risks such as bias, privacy violations, and a lack of accountability— ensuring that AI technology works for everyone, not just select groups.

Moreover, international collaboration on AI technologies can help harmonize standards, reduce fragmentation, and build a cohesive global framework. Such efforts can lead to shared advancements and mutual trust, facilitating the seamless integration of AI across borders. Countries that invest in inclusive AI ecosystems—promoting educational initiatives, developing robust data infrastructures, and supporting policies—are not only leading technologically but are also fostering trust and unity.

Cultural sensitivity in AI deployment is also pivotal. By respecting and integrating diverse cultural and ethical perspectives, AI can help unify fractured societies. This approach bolsters local trust and allows for global AI strategies that accommodate varied norms and expectations, making AI a tool of unity rather than division.

In essence, achieving AI-infused cohesion requires a commitment to ethical integrity, international cooperation, and inclusivity. These pillars provide the foundation for building trust in AI, encouraging collective progress, and fostering a united technological landscape. For AI to reach its full potential in creating a cohesive society, it must be implemented with care, respect, and a shared vision for a connected future. Retaining our focus on societal political fragmentation, let's turn the page and begin the long road home.

Chapter 13
The Long Road Home

In the authors' recently-released "tome" titled *Reblooming the Knowledge Movement: The Democratization of Organizations*, we focused on achieving resonance and coherence as key concepts in organizational behavior and culture. Resonance refers to the level of connection between the organization and its employees (in a democracy, the government and its citizens) and the alignment of individual group goals, values, and behaviors (which per the early philosophers includes, at the societal level, freedoms and liberties, individual rights and responsibilities, participation, equal opportunity based on merit, distribution of wealth, a coercive-free environment, rational consensus, and choice to pursue a good life). This requires decisions and actions based on truth, trust, reason, rationality, mutual respect, and good will. It also recognizes the need for—along with the "collision of adverse opinions" in the search for higher truth—cooperation, collaboration, and open dialogue. To widen our perspective, let's briefly look at and learn from fragmentation through the lens of quantum theory.

DALL-E representation of quantum fragmentation.

In quantum physics, the idea of fragmentation can be seen in the concept of quantum *decoherence and entanglement*, where particles exist in a superposition of states until measured. [*Reference:* Nielsen, M. A., & Chuag, I.L. (2000). *Quantum Computation and Quantum Information.* Cambridge University Press.]

Fragmentation is inherent in the quantum world, where different states and probabilities coexist. This fragmentation allows for diverse outcomes and possibilities, fostering innovation and discovery in fields such as quantum computing, where multiple states can be processed simultaneously, vastly increasing computational power and efficiency. [*Reference:* Zurek, W. H. (200). Decoherence, Einselection, and the Quantum Origins of the Classical. *Reviews of Modern Physics, 75(3), 715.*]

Emerging as powerful tools in the chaotic uncertain environment of today's world, where in quantum terms all things are possible and it is our choices that ultimately confine and refine our thought, Knowledge Capacities enable our minds to shift our views and perceptions of emerging challenges in our search of solutions. Capacity—referring to the broad potential or inherent ability of individuals and organizations to learn, adapt, and grow over time—is much larger than capability, which refers to specific skills, competencies and knowledge to perform particular tasks for functions effectively within a given context.

Knowledge Capacities, supporting Whole Thought, encompass the fundamental ways of thinking, being, and acting that allow one to effectively engage with dynamic and complex environments. As researchers, we engage several KCs in our pursuit of healing and building on the fragmented pieces of our erupting world at the societal level. The first simple approach is reversal, which was the KC that was initially recognized and successfully applied some 35 years ago by the Acquisition Reform Executive in the U.S. Department of the Navy. Along with critical and creative thinking, we also engage Metasystemic Thinking, Limitless Potential Expansion, Pattern Perception, and Thought Experimentation, all available as open source materials (see www.kmrom.com/knowledge-capacities for downloads). [*Reference:* Bennet, A., & Turner, R. (2024). *Whole Thought: The Rise of Human Intelligence.* MQIPress.]

We also build on the Intelligent Complex Adaptive System model for organizations, recognizing that we and our organizations, and as a global entity, are complex adaptive systems *with the potential to act intelligently.* Keeping this in mind, we begin with what we have so far learned together in this book.

[*Reference:* Bennet, A., & Bennet, D. (2004). *Organizational Survival in the New World: The Intelligent Complex Adaptive Organization*. Elsevier.]

Addressing Societal Political Fragmentation

First, regardless of the reasons, if a government intentionally aimed to fragment society, it would seek to undermine or dismantle the structures and practices that traditionally *promote social cohesion and unity*. Building on our earlier exploration, the actions this would involve are listed in the left column. In the right column, counter factors are identified that would stabilize the fragmented society and seed the social journey toward resonance and cohesion.

Fragmentation Factors of Structures and Practices that Promote Social Cohesion and Unity	Counter Factors to Stabilize and Seed Resonance & Coherence
ENCOURAGING POLITICAL POLARIZATION **Exploiting Divisions:** Amplifying political divides through rhetoric or policy choices that pit groups against each other. Encouraging campaigns of misinformation that bolster extreme political identities and discourage moderate viewpoints. **Undermining Political Dialogue:** Disrupting forums and processes designed for bipartisan or multiparty dialogue could prevent consensus-building. Using social media to exacerbate polarization through algorithms that favor sensationalist and partisan content.	**Promote Inclusive Dialogue:** Facilitate bipartisan and cross-cultural forums that encourage understanding and compromise across political divides. **Grassroots and Community Engagement:** Form local, nonpartisan groups focused on community projects that benefit everyone, building relationships across divides. **Parallel Dialogues:** Establish citizen platforms for dialogue, such as town halls or online forums, where diverse voices can engage constructively on common concerns **Strengthen Political Institutions:** Invest in restoring and enhancing platforms for political dialogue that actively include diverse viewpoints and promote consensus-building
EXACERBATING ECONOMIC INEQUALITY **Unequal Resource Distribution:** Implementing policies that widen the gap between wealthy and poorer citizens can create further economic divisions, leading to social unrest. Incorporating examples of tax benefits like healthcare and education that further entrench inequality. **Reducing Support for Social Safety Nets:** Withdrawing support from programs that level the playing field, such as education and healthcare, would likely deepen social divides. Emphasizing the impact of privatizing essential services, which limits access for lower-income groups.	Implement Equitable Policies: Develop policies that ensure fair distribution of resources, such as progressive taxation and closing loopholes that favor the wealthy. Invest in Social Programs: Reinstate and expand funding for education, healthcare, and other social services to level the playing field and reduce inequality. Community-Based Economic Initiatives: Develop local cooperatives and support networks that provide resources and opportunities for disadvantaged groups. Nonprofit and NGO Involvement: Encourage local nonprofits and international NGOs to fill gaps in social services and advocate for policy change.
UNDERMINING INCLUSIVITY AND DIVERSITY **Discrimination and Exclusion:** Implementing policies or practices that discriminate against or	**Enhance Anti-Discrimination Laws:** Strengthen legal protections and affirmative actions that

exclude minority to create divisions fostering resentment and social tensions. Using systemic racism and institutional biases to perpetuate discrimination.

Promoting Uniformity over Diversity: Suppressing cultural, religious, or ethnic diversity to marginalize minority groups and erode societal cohesion. Leads to feelings of alienation and division. Implement nationalist or isolationist policies to stoke fears of the "other".

Discouraging Multicultural Initiatives: Reducing support for multiculturalism and diversity initiatives limits cultural expression and opportunities for different groups to engage positively. Restricting platforms that support multicultural expression and interaction can lead to cultural isolation and prevent the integration of diverse perspectives. Subjugating diverse histories and contributions.

Undermining Anti-Discrimination Efforts: Weakening and reducing legal and institutional protections against discrimination to increase bias and inequality, deepening societal fractures. Rollbacking of laws and policies protecting LGBTQ+ communities, immigrants, and other vulnerable groups.

WEAKENING INSTITUTIONS

Destabilizing Public Institutions: Eroding trust in key institutions like the judiciary or media can increase social fragmentation by reducing their effectiveness and perceived legitimacy. Ensuring political interference in judiciary and media to undermine their independence.

Restricting Civic Participation: Limiting opportunities for civic engagement or dismantling platforms for community involvement could lead to greater societal disconnection. Implementing voter suppression tactics and restrictive electoral practices to limit participation.

RESTRICTING EDUCATION AND CIVIC ENGAGEMENT

Controlling Education Content: Manipulating educational content to diminish critical thinking or promoting biased narratives may fragment intellectual unity and understanding. Engaging in censorship and banning books that present diverse perspectives.

Cutting Funding to Education Programs: Using University research grants as bargaining chips for autocrat's agenda. Eliminating government funding and student loan

promote equality and representation of marginalized groups.

Celebrate Diversity: Encourage policies and initiatives that highlight the cultural, ethnic, and religious diversity of the society as a source of strength. Host cultural festivals and educational campaigns that highlight and celebrate diversity, fostering a shared community identity.

Support Multicultural Initiatives: Invest in programs that promote multicultural education and interaction to foster mutual respect and understanding. Organize exchange programs and partnerships between diverse groups to encourage mutual understanding and collaboration.

Seek Support from Corporations and Philanthropists: Engage businesses and philanthropists to fund and promote multicultural initiatives.

Reinforce Legal Protection: Enhance legal frameworks and enforcement against discrimination to promote equality and societal cohesion. Form coalitions of legal advocates to protect rights through existing legal frameworks and international human rights channels.

Strengthen Institutional Integrity: Build transparency and accountability in public institutions to restore trust and their effectiveness.

Promote Civic Engagement: Invest in civic education and create more opportunities for citizen involvement at all levels of government.

Public Campaigns for Trust-Building: Run campaigns that highlight the importance of institutional trust and feature success stories where institutions work effectively.

Promote Voter Participation and Education: Conduct awareness drives and workshops on the importance of voting and civic engagement, even when electoral systems seem compromised.

Encourage Critical Thinking: Ensure educational content promotes diverse perspectives and critical thinking, not biased narratives.

Increase Educational Investment: Restore and boost funding for education programs and institutions to ensure equal access and opportunities for all.

Enhance Civic Education: Integrate comprehensive civic education into curriculums to promote informed citizenship and active participation in democracy.

Independent Educational Resources: Develop open-access educational materials and online courses that offer balanced perspectives and foster opportunities. Limit educational and future opportunities for disadvantaged communities.

Reducing Civic Education: Limiting opportunities for civic engagement or dismantling platforms for community involvement could lead to greater societal disconnection. Removing or diluting programs promoting democratic values.

creative and critical thinking. Encourage participation in open resources such as Kahn Academy or Knowledge Capacities.

Community-Funded Scholarships: Establish scholarship programs funded by local businesses and community members to support underserved students.

Informal Civic Education Projects: Launch community groups focused on teaching civic values and skills, using local media and social events

PROMOTING EXCLUSIVE NARRATIVES

Propagating Exclusive Ideologies: Promoting narratives that favor a specific group or ideology alienates others, fostering an us-versus-them mentality. Embed algorithmic bias in spreading specific narratives.

Divisive Media Campaign: Using media to propagate divisive narratives and misinformation can deepen societal divides and create echo chambers. Enable foreign interference and funding to help shape divisive narratives.

Promote Media Literacy: Introduce media literacy programs that empower individuals to analyze and engage with media content critically. Create grassroots workshops and online resources teaching media literacy to help people critically assess the information they encounter

Foster Ethical Journalism: Support independent media organizations that adhere to high standards of ethical journalism and balanced reporting. Support independent media outlets and journalists who are committed to ethical standards and diverse narratives.

LEGAL AND JUDICIAL POLICIES

Manipulating Legal Frameworks: Altering legislation to benefit specific groups or interests to erode the public's trust I the rule of law.

Judicial Independence: Undermining the independence and impartiality of the judiciary through political pressure or biased appointments to compromise the justice system's fairness.

Ensure Legal Fairness: Reform legal systems to protect them from manipulation, ensuring fair and equal treatment for all under the law.

Protect Judicial Autonomy and Support Judicial integrity: Ensure the judiciary is free from political influence through transparent appointment processes and secure tenure. Advocate for the protection of judicial independence through international pressure and partnerships with global legal entities.

International Partnerships: Work with international human rights organizations to monitor and report legal injustices, gaining international support and intervention.

GOVERNMENT TRANSPARENCY AND ACCOUNTABILITY

Erosion of Transparency: Reducing transparency in government processes and decision-making to breed mistrust and disengagement among citizens. Conducting significant policy decision behind closed doors without public consultation or oversight.

Lack of Accountability Mechanisms: Weakening structures that hold government official accountable, leading to corruption and weakening public confidence in governance. Dismantling or undermining institutions that investigate and penalize government misconduct.

Enhance Government Openness: Implement open data initiatives and transparency measures for government activities to boost public trust.

Strengthen Accountability Structures: Establish independent oversight bodies to ensure that government officials are held accountable for their actions.

Citizen Monitoring Groups: Create watchdog groups to monitor government activities and promote transparency through social media and other public forums.

International Alliances: Leverage international bodies to sanction or pressure regimes that undermine accountability, using global platforms to highlight these issues.

The Long Road Home:
Bringing social cohesion to societal fragmentation.

By implementing these countermeasures, it's possible to address the various areas of fragmentation and work toward a more stable, cohesive society that values inclusivity, fairness, and open dialogue. Further, each of these strategies includes a focus on building local and global networks of accountability and support, fostering resilience and cohesion even when direct governmental change is not immediately possible. While we have used the example of societal fragmentation, this same approach can be applied to other fragmentation domains to search out solutions.

I, Me, the Individual

Continuing with our focus on addressing societal political fragmentation, as an individual there are several valuable ways you can contribute to fostering social cohesion and addressing societal fragmentation. These actions are geared toward bridging the divides among people and contributing to a more unified, cohesive society. Your individual efforts, combined with those of others, can collectively drive meaningful change.

First, **engage locally**. *Volunteer*: Join local community organizations or participate in activities that address social issues, such as food banks or neighborhood clean-ups. *Support Local Businesses:* Encourage economic resilience by purchasing from local vendors and supporting community-owned enterprises.

Second, **foster dialogue.** *Host Conversations:* Organize discussions or book clubs that explore diverse perspectives and encourage empathy, that which is the fundamental strength of Western Civilization. *Be an Active Listener:* Cultivate the habit of listening to others with different views, seeking to understand rather than to argue.

Third, **educate and inform**. *Share Responsible Information*: Use your social media platforms to share accurate, well-sourced information and promote media literacy among your networks. *Infinite Learning:* Continuously educate yourself on social, political, and economic issues to better understand complexities and advocate for change.

Fourth, **promote inclusivity**. *Champion Diversity:* Support initiatives that promote inclusion within your workplace, schools, and community. *Mentorship:* Mentor individuals from marginalized communities, offering guidance and support to help them achieve their goals.

Fifth, **advocate for change**. *Participate in Civic Activities:* Vote in elections, attend town hall meetings, and engage in peaceful advocacy campaigns on issues you care about. *Support Advocacy Groups:* Back organizations working to address the root causes of social fragmentation through donations or volunteer work.

Sixth, **build networks**. *Connect with Others:* Develop relationships with people from varied backgrounds to build understanding and community support networks. *Collaborate:* Work with others on projects or initiatives that promote the common good, pooling resources and ideas

Seventh, **practice resilience and empathy**. *Model Positive Behavior:* Exhibit empathy, patience, and resilience in your interactions, setting an example for others. *Self-Care:* Maintain your well-being to stay engaged and effective in your efforts, ensuring you have the energy and capacity to contribute positively.

Now, let's explore how we might approach *applying* all of this learning both collectively and individually.

The Resilient Societal Cohesion Model

Moving from shattered to unity is enabled by an effective change process. The RSCM model is (a) grounded in fostering personal and collective resilience, focusing on cultivating qualities that counteract societal fragmentation, and (b)

integrating strategies for dealing with fragmentation while promoting cohesion. While both (a) and (b) can—and should—be advanced simultaneously, it is important to emphasize the importance of both as part of the long road home.

In a democracy, each and every individual is important and has something to contribute to the larger whole. Thus, nurturing ourselves, empowering ourselves, is critical to building and expanding cohesion across a fragmented society. You will notice that empowerment, both in terms of the individual and the collective, that is, coming from within ourselves and as support from the groups within which we act, is placed at the beginning and end of the model.

Empowerment enriches democracy by enabling more comprehensive and meaningful participation, and democracy provides a structure that supports and enhances empowerment efforts. Key aspects of that relationship are participation and inclusion, agency and autonomy, accountability and transparency, social justice and equality, education and awareness, and community development. In short, empowerment is vital to addressing the challenges of fragmentation.

Let's take a close look at the RSCM model.

A. Fostering Personal and Collective Resilience

A-1. Individual Empowerment. *Inner Development:* Cultivate qualities like compassion, humility, and integrity through self-reflection, education, and personal growth. *Resilience Building:* Embrace and engage Emotional Intelligence and develop Knowledge Capacities to build emotional and social resilience, enabling you to withstand external pressures and respond to emerging uncertainties.

Relevant Knowledge Capacities (available as open source materials from KMROM www.kmrom.com/knowledge-capaccities) include: Adaptive Resilience, Cognitive Empathy, Cultivating Humility, Empathic Engagement, Expanding Human Algorithms, Limitless Potential Expansion, Self-Efficacy Empowerment, and Unbounded Adaption.

[*References:* Goleman, D. (2005). *Emotional Intelligence: Why It Can Matter More than IQ*. Bantam. Also, Bennet, A., & Turner, R. (2024). *Knowledge Capacities: Igniting Whole Thought*. MQIPress. Also, Turner, R., & Bennet, A. (2024). *Knowledge Capacities II: Cultivating Infinite Learning*. MQIPress.]

A-2. Community Engagement. *Support Networks:* Foster community bonds by creating local networks that encourage dialogue, shared activities, and mutual support. *Collective Action:* Promote community-driven initiatives that address shared challenges and enhance societal cohesion, focusing on inclusivity and diversity.

A-3. Institutional Support. *Inclusive Policies:* Encourage institutions to adopt policies that support social safety nets and promote equity, ensuring that diverse voices are heard and valued. *Transparency and Trust-Building:* Strengthen institutional integrity by ensuring decision-making processes are transparent and accountable to the community.

A-4. Infinite Learning and Adaptation. *Curiosity and Innovation:* Encourage an environment where continuous learning is valued, promoting the exploration of diverse ideas and solutions to societal problems. *Recognition of Self:* Fully engage your vast conscious, unconscious, and social learning resources. *Feedback Loops:* Implement systems that allow for ongoing feedback and adaptation, ensuring that individuals and communities can learn from experiences and adjust strategies accordingly.

[*Reference:* Bennet, A. (2024). *Infinite Learning: Your Life, Your Choice.* MQIPress.]

A-5. Global and Local Integration. *Harmonize Initiatives:* Align local community efforts with broader global movements and policies, ensuring a unified approach to addressing common challenges. *Cultural Exchange:* Promote opportunities for cultural exchange and understanding both locally and internationally, to enhance empathy and respect across different groups.

B. Fragmentation Integration

B-1. Recognize and Address Fragmentation. *Identify Areas of Disunity:* Map out societal divisions—be they political, economic, cultural, or institutional—and acknowledge the underlying causes of these fragmentations. *Targeted Interventions:* Develop specific strategies to address and mend the gaps in these areas, focusing efforts where fragmentation is most acute.

B-2. Dialogue and Mediation. *Constructive Conversations:* Set up platforms for dialogue involving all stakeholders, aiming to bridge divides by fostering understanding and collaboration. *Targeted Interventions:* Develop specific strategies to address and mend the gaps in these areas, focusing efforts where fragmentation is most acute.

B-3. Integrate Fragmented Networks. *Cross-Community Initiatives:* Establish initiatives that bring together disparate groups, focusing on shared interests and goals to build bridges. *Diverse Collaboration:*

Encourage collaborations that include diverse voices, ensuring that solutions reflect the needs and perspectives of all societal sectors.

B-4. Leverage Technology for Connection. *Digital Platforms for Inclusion:* Use technology to connect communities, provide information, and facilitate inclusive discussions that transcend geographical and social barriers. *Combat Misinformation:* Use technology to connect communities, provide information, and facilitate inclusive discussions that transcend geographical and social barriers.

B-5. Role of Individuals in Repairing Fragmentation. Micro-Level Actions: Empower individuals to take small, meaningful actions within their circles, such as fostering inclusive dialogues or engaging in community service. *Amplify Positive Narratives.* Encourage storytelling that highlights successful resolutions of conflict and showcases unity in diversity.

Part A of the RSCM model leverages individual qualities and community dynamics as foundational elements for creating a resilient, cohesive society. By focusing on empowerment, engagement, and infinite learning, the model aims to stabilize and unify diverse elements within the broader social fabric. Part B of the RSCM model directly addresses fragmentation while promoting qualities that foster cohesion, aiming to provide a more comprehensive approach to healing societal divides and building lasting unity.

While the path toward social cohesion may seem daunting in the face of persistent fragmentation, it is through concerted individual and collective efforts that meaningful change can be realized. By engaging actively within our communities, fostering open dialogue, and embracing diversity, each of us can contribute to a more inclusive and resilient society. The journey toward unity requires patience, empathy, and an unwavering commitment to understanding and supporting one another. As we continue to advocate for equitable policies and participate in civic responsibilities, we lay the groundwork for a future where collaboration and shared purpose transcend divisions. Ultimately, it is the unwavering spirit of individuals, acting with integrity and purpose, that will chart the long road home toward a harmonious and interconnected world.

Chapter 14
The Glimmer of Light

In the tapestry of life, each of us holds a mirror to the world around us. The notion that our scattered thoughts can reflect the complexities and fragmentation of the larger world is not just metaphorical; it's a lived experience. Thus the mental/emotional domain is entangled with fragmentation at every level.

Like pieces of a puzzle laid across the table of our minds, our thoughts scatter under the pressures of modern life, embodying the same fragmentation we see in the environment, in technology, and within societies. As we navigate these personal challenges, our experiences become microcosms of the greater world, revealing profound insights that can guide us toward understanding and unity.

Sarah, a graphic designer, finds her creativity fragmented by a barrage of project deadlines and digital distractions. Her mind is a kaleidoscope, spinning with vibrant yet disjointed ideas. One day, as she takes a pause in a serene park, she witnesses a flock of birds moving with effortless coherence. Inspired, Sarah begins to see her scattered thoughts not as obstacles but as potential catalysts for aligning her creative energies. Her personal journey mirrors the world's flux, suggesting that harmony can arise from chaos.

Derek, inundated by the cacophony of digital notifications, feels his focus dissipating in the fragmented realm of social media and news feeds. The digital landscape, once a source of connection, now mirrors his internal struggle for clarity. Choosing to step away, Derek embarks on digital detoxification, using the time to weave threads of cohesive understanding from a tapestry of scattered information. His experience highlights the power of intentionality in navigating a fragmented digital world.

These narratives illustrate that individual experiences of fragmentation reflect broader global complexities—be it in our creativity, our digital interactions, or our emotional landscapes.

Inner Reflection of a Fragmented World

The human appears to have a natural ability to process and benefit from fragmentation. This is not surprising. Individuals function as complex adaptive systems within larger societal contexts, with dynamic processes that govern personal growth and adaptation, mirroring the challenges and opportunities present in complex systems. Let's explore this a bit further.

CAS Relationship to Fragmentation

As a CAS, we adjust to new information, experiences, and environments, even when we are averse to change. This adaptability is influenced by the different physical, mental, and emotional "fragments" of a person, each contributing to how they navigate change. For example, Holland's work on adaptive systems discusses mechanisms through which components alter behavior in response to environmental changes, akin to human adaptation in learning and growth. Specifically, how systems made up of individual "fragments" or components— each with its own set of rules and behaviors—can collectively develop adaptability and resilience. [*Reference:* Holland, J. H. (1992). *Adaptation in Natural and Artificial Systems: An Introductory Analysis with Applications to Biology, Control, and Artificial Intelligence*. MIT Press.]

Fragmentation doesn't just pose challenges; it also contributes to emergent properties, where the whole is greater than the sum of its parts. Fragmentation facilitates the breakdown of a system into diverse physical, mental, and emotional fragments, setting the stage for development of emergent properties, which can lead to new insights, innovative thinking and creative problem-solving. Diverse fragments lead to a rich pool of resources and perspectives which, when integrated effectively, lead to outcomes that would not have been possible if each fragment functioned independently. [*Reference:* Bennet, D. (2023). Systems and Complexity Thinking. In A. Bennet & R. Turner, *Reblooming the Knowledge Movement: The Democratization of Organizations*. MQIPress.]

Further, a CAS often demonstrates self-organizing capabilities, where order and structure emerge without centralized control. Humans exhibit self-organizing behaviors by learning to integrate fragmented aspects of themselves to achieve personal coherence and stability. As described by Kauffman, self-organization is crucial in both biological and social systems when processing societal fragmentation. In biological systems, self-organization refers to the process by which structure and order arise spontaneously form the interactions among simpler components without the need for a central governing authority. These capacities are crucial for robustness and resilience, innovation and evolution, adaptation to change, and emergence of complex structures and patterns. In societal systems, this means that collective behaviors and institutions can emerge organically, helping to reintegrate fragmented elements into a cohesive whole. [*Reference:* Kauffman, S. (1993). *The Origins of Order: Self-Organization and Selection in Evolution*. Oxford University Press.]

Both the human as an ICALS (intelligent complex adaptive learning system) and the organization as an ICAS (intelligent complex adaptive system) share characteristics of nonlinearity. Small changes in one aspect of a person can lead to unforeseen and significant impacts across other areas, an attribute of complex adaptive systems. This nonlinearity explains why personal development can be unpredictable and varied among individuals. It also explains why the human response to fragmented societal systems is itself fragmented. [*Reference:* Capra, F. (1996). *The Web of Life: A New Scientific Understanding of Living Systems*. Anchor Books.]

Through the lens of nonlinearity, fragmentation is not just seen as a breakdown of order but as an opportunity for complexity, adaptation, and new growth trajectories. First, in *unpredictable outcomes*. When a system or individual experiences a fragmented input (new experience, change, internal emotional shifts), the resulting adjustments can be vastly different from expectations. Second, related to *interconnectedness and ripple effects*.

Fragmentation often implies that components of a system are partially disconnected or operating independently. However, because of the nonlinear nature of a CAS, changes in one fragment can ripple across the entire system, causing adjustments and adaptations in unexpected ways. This interconnectedness, despite apparent fragmentation, highlights the complex web of influences within adaptive systems.

Third, in the *emergence of complexity*, building on the adage complexity begets complexity, just as fragmentation begets fragmentation. Nonlinearity allows for the emergence of new patterns and complex behaviors from seemingly simple and fragmented components. As these components interact, they can spontaneously self-organize into more sophisticated structures, demonstrating resilience and adaptability in both individual and organizational contexts. Fourth, through *diverse trajectories of development*. In human systems, individual fragments (mental, emotional, physical) might respond differently to the same stimulus due to nonlinearity. This results in a broad spectrum of developmental paths and coping mechanisms, reflecting the personalized ways each person integrates and reacts to fragmentation within themselves and their environment.

In an ICAS organization, feedback loops help systems adjust and maintain equilibrium, and they have a central role in our individuals and organizations navigate fragmentation. Both an ICAS and ICALS (Intelligent Complex Adaptive Learning Systems) (humans) receive feedback from their environment, which facilitates learning and can influence physical, mental, and emotional states. Feedback loops can be either positive or negative. Positive feedback amplifies changes or growth, potentially exacerbating fragmentation if not managed carefully. Negative feedback, on the other hand, aims to restore balance and stability, often working to integrate fragmented elements back into a coherent whole.

Further, feedback loops are ongoing and cyclical, meaning they don't just influence a system once but continue to affect it in a loop. This cyclic nature helps maintain dynamic stability within systems, even amid fragmentation. As environments and situations change, feedback loops help systems recalibrate continuously, integrating fragmented parts over time. Pragmatically, feedback loops help in finding a balance between beneficial fragmentation (which can foster innovation and diversity) and necessary cohesion (which ensures functionality and common purpose). Recognizing the tension and interplay between these aspects can guide both personal growth and organizational strategy.

As can be seen, feedback loops not only help in maintaining equilibrium but also act as mechanisms through which fragmentation and integration occur. Thus, we recognize that the external recognition of fragmentation and the individual human internal response to physical, mental and emotional fragmentation are entangled. But there is more. We are simultaneously processing information from internal sources.

Going Deeper: Fragmentation of the Human Soul

In *The Fragmentation of Being*—the most in depth treatment available on the fragmentation of the human soul—Kris McDaniel challenges conventional ideas about what it means to exist. By introducing the notion of fragmentation within existence, he provides a new framework for understanding the complexities of being, the complexities of self. He argues against the traditional view that existence is univocal, meaning that everything that exists does so in the same way. Instead, he proposes that there are different modes of being, suggesting a more fragmented understanding of existence. Being is not a monolithic concept but is rather fragmented into different kinds of degrees. This fragmentation challenges the notion of a single, unified account of existence, encouraging a more nuanced understanding of reality. [*Reference:* McDaniel, K. (2017). *The Fragmentation of the Soul.* Oxford.]

To a certain extent the physical/mental/emotional human that traverses this world reflects the fragmentation of the soul described by McDaniel. As we have reflected above, the very concept of fragmentation in the context of the physical, mental and emotional aspects of an individual is consistent with our understanding of people as complex adaptive systems, hopefully intelligent ones. Human beings are complex entities with multiple dimensions to their existence, each encompassing different experiences, needs, and expressions.

It is a short step to consider the influence of the fragmentation of the human soul across the holistic human. In exploring the individual from this point of view, *physical fragmentation* could refer to how our physical bodies can be understood and analyzed in various ways. Physiological processes, health, fitness, and physical attributes all contribute to our physical identity but do not fully encompass who we are. As various challenges present themselves to the physical condition throughout life, there is no doubt that there are specific periods of fragmentation.

Mental fragmentation would refer to our thoughts, beliefs, cognitive processes, and mental states that contribute to our intellectual identity. However, these aspects can be in conflict or evolve over time, reflecting a fragmented intellectual landscape. *Emotional fragmentation* recognizes the significant role emotions play in our identity and experiences. Emotional fragmentation might manifest in experiencing contradictory emotions simultaneously or feeling disconnected from one's emotional responses.

While these aspects can feel fragmented, humans typically strive for a sense of integration or harmony. Personal growth, self-awareness, and holistic approaches to health and well-being aim to acknowledge and integrate these fragments into a cohesive sense of self. That cohesive sense of self is a product of our consciousness, whose role is to tie our life together into a coherent story. Moving through various life experiences, the individual singles out and accentuates what is significant and connects these events to historic events to create a narrative unity, what can be described as a fictionalized history. This autobiographical self—the idea of who we are, the image we build up of ourselves and where we fit socially—is built up over years of experience and constantly being remodeled, a product of infinite learning in an experiential life. [*Reference*: Bennet, D., Bennet, A., & Turner, R. (2023). *Unleashing the Human Mind: A Consilience Approach to Managing Self*. MQIPress.]

The fragmentation that occurs in our physical, mental, and emotional dimensions, a reflection of the fragmentation of the soul, can present internal challenges, just as physical, digital and societal fragmentation presents challenges in our external world. For example, fragmentation often results in internal conflicts—conflicting desires, beliefs, or emotions. These conflicts can create inner turmoil, making it difficult to make decisions or maintain focus. One's emotional response to a situation might be at odds with logical reasoning, leading to stress or anxiety. Emotional fragmentation, especially when unresolved, can lead to overwhelming feelings that inhibit learning and development. Managing emotions becomes a priority, which can detract from focusing on educational or developmental goals.

Connecting the idea of fragmentation in our physical, mental, and emotional lives to the concept of "soul fragmentation" can provide a rich metaphor for understanding personal development and the complexities of human identity, and may offer guidance for handling societal fragmentation. Let's develop a case for how these aspects might reflect and influence each other.

Just as the soul is often thought of as the core essence of a person, influencing and integrating all facets of existence, fragmentation in our physical, mental, and emotional lives might mirror deep-seated discordances within this core. When the soul—or our innermost values and sense of self—is not harmonized, it might manifest as fragmentation in how we experience the world. In essence, the fragmentation of the soul can symbolize a split or divergence within our deepest selves, leading to inconsistencies in our outer lives. If one's soul is perceived to be in disarray or conflict, this might be reflected in the way we experience our thoughts, emotions, and physical states, creating a feedback loop where inner unrest manifests externally.

This inner unrest often centers around existential questions related to self. For example, a corporate executive who, despite achieving all career goals, feels unfulfilled and questions the meaningfulness of daily routines and material success. [*Reference:* Frankl, V. E. (1959). *Man's Search for Meaning.* Beacon Press.] This may also involve dissociation experiences. For example, during a stressful meeting, a person might suddenly feel disconnected, as if watching the meeting unfold from outside their body, unable to engage with the discussion. [*Reference:* Herman, J. (1992). *Trauma and Recovery: The Aftermath of Violence—From Domestic Abuse to Political Terror.* Basic Books.]

Here's how these ideas can be interconnected:

Disconnection from Inner Self: Soul fragmentation implies a separation or disconnection from integral aspects of one's being. This can lead to identity confusion because the person may not have a cohesive understanding of who they are at their core, leading to uncertainty and inconsistency in how they see themselves and how they present to the world.

Trauma and Identity: Experiences that might cause soul fragmentation, such as trauma or significant life changes, can disrupt one's sense of identity. When parts of the self are emotionally or psychologically inaccessible, it becomes challenging to maintain a unified sense of identity. This can result in confusion over personal beliefs, values, and goals.

Search for Meaning: In many spiritual and psychological perspectives, part of finding one's identity involves integrating various life experiences, emotions, and aspects of the self into a coherent whole. Soul fragmentation can make this integration difficult, leading individuals to continually search for external sources of validation or meaning in an attempt to piece together a fragmented self-image.

Role of the Subconscious: Sometimes, elements of the self that are not fully acknowledged or integrated reside in the subconscious, influencing behaviors and feelings without explicit awareness. This lack of awareness can foster identity confusion, as the individual may not understand the root of their conflicts or inconsistencies.

From these perspectives the fragmentation of the soul can be seen as a *disruptive force necessitating adaptation*. Intelligent complex adaptive systems require adjustments to thrive; humans are prompted by soul fragmentation to find new ways of integrating their physical, mental, and emotional selves with their perceived physical reality.

By now, we recognize that moving through societal fragmentation is a search for coherence and unity. This mirrors the process individuals undergo in reconciling disparate aspects of their physical, mental, and emotional lives. Pursuing wholeness in our internal existence could lead to a more unified and harmonious external existence.

Fragmentation of the Human Soul

The Glimmer

From the above discussion, it is reasonable to propose that *humans have an innate ability to navigate through societal fragmentation*. This ability can be understood through several lenses:

1. **Adaptive Capacity.** As intelligent complex adaptive systems, individuals have the capacity to learn and adjust in response to their environment. This adaptability includes both personal and collective dimensions, allowing societies to evolve and address fragmentation over time.

2. **Innate Resilience.** Humans possess a natural resilience that enables them to cope with, and often thrive in, challenging and fragmented environments. Social cohesion, empathy, and communication are innate human skills that play pivotal roles in overcoming division.

3. **Capacity for Understanding and Empathy.** The human ability to understand and empathize with others fosters connection, even amid societal divisions. This capacity is crucial for bridging gaps between different groups and promoting unity.

4. **Cultural and Historical Precedents.** History is replete with examples of societies overcoming fragmentation. Humans have a track record of forming new alliances, engaging in dialogue, and finding common ground, suggesting an intrinsic capability to mend divisions.

5. **Shared Values and Goals.** Despite fragmentation, people often share common values and goals, such as security, well-being, and prosperity. These shared aspirations can serve as a foundation for collaborative efforts to address and reduce societal divides.

6. **Innovation and Problem Solving.** Human ingenuity and creativity are key assets in devising solutions to complex problems, including those posed by societal fragmentation. Collaborative problem-solving and innovation can help bridge divides.

While fragmentation presents significant challenges, these inherent human capacities provide a pathway toward greater cohesion and unity. However, as intelligent complex adaptive systems, there is more to consider related to potential qualities of being human.

The Echo Within

Throughout this book there are human qualities that have repeatedly emerged in our discussions of processing fragmentation and moving toward coherence. No doubt you have observed these as well, and reflect many of them in your thought, feelings and actions. These are compassion, humility, empathy, patience, respect, integrity, curiosity, forgiveness and harmonism. While this set of human qualities is no doubt incomplete, it emerges as a reflection of potentialities as humanity moves into the future. Let's take a closer look at these human qualities and their relationship to fragmentation.

Compassion. This quality ensures that policies and societal structures remain centered around human well-being. Compassion drives leaders and citizens alike to understand the broader impact of their actions and decisions, leading to societies that are more inclusive and protective of all individuals, especially the most vulnerable. [*Reference:* Levine, D. A., (2005). *Teaching Empathy: A Blueprint for Caring, Compassion, and Community*. Solution Tree.]

Humility. By acknowledging our limitations and opening to the thoughts of others, humility makes room for continuous learning and adaptation. This openness is critical in a world of diverse perspectives and challenges, enabling leaders to draw from a collective pool of knowledge to craft informed and context-sensitive approaches to social issues. [Hess, E. D., & Ludwig, K. (2017). *Humility is the New Smart: Rethinking Excellence in the Smart Machine Age*. Berrett-Koehler Publishers.]

Empathy. Empathy serves as a powerful tool for bridging divides. By understanding and valuing the experiences of others, societies can develop policies and practices that are not only equitable but also resonate with all community members. Empathy fosters solidarity by focusing on shared human experiences. [*Reference:* Krznaric, R. (2014). *Empathy: A Handbook for Revolution*. Random House.]

Patience. Societal cohesion often requires time to build. Patience encourages careful reflection and nurtures sustainable solutions that can withstand the test of time. Through patience, societies can develop layered strategies that thoughtfully integrate multiple viewpoints and interests, avoiding shortsighted fixes. [*Reference:* Ryan, M. J. (2003). The Power of Patience: *How This Old-Fashioned Virtue Can Improve Your Life*. Conari Press.]

Respect. By valuing every voice, respect fuels inclusive decision-making. It establishes a platform where all stakeholders can contribute meaningfully, leading to more comprehensive and accepted solutions. Respect highlights the importance of diversity as a strength rather than a dividing factor. [*Reference:* Meshanko, P. (2013). *The Respect Effect: Using the Science of Neuroleadership to Inspire a More Loyal and Productive Workplace*. McGraw-Hill Education.]

Integrity. Trust is the bedrock of social cohesion, and integrity ensures that trust is well-placed. Through honest and ethical governance, integrity fosters confidence in institutions and policies, enhancing communal faith in shared goals and fairness. [*Reference:* Cloud, H. (2006). *Integrity: the Courage to Meet the Demands of Reality*. Harper Collins.]

Curiosity. This quality drives innovation and the discovery of novel solutions. With curiosity, societies can explore new ideas that may better address underlying issues of fragmentation while simultaneously encouraging a culture of lifelong learning and adaptation. [*Reference:* Berger, W. (2014). *A More Beautiful Question: The Power of Inquiry to Spark Breakthrough Ideas*. Bloomsbury USA.]

Forgiveness. Mistakes are inevitable, but how they are handled can either divide or unite. Forgiveness promotes resilience and collaboration, encouraging a culture where errors are seen as learning opportunities. By prioritizing growth over blame, societies can heal and strengthen bonds. *Reference:* McCullough, M.E. (2008). *Beyond Revenge: The Evolution of the Forgiveness Instinct*. Jossey-Bass.]

Harmonism. Striving for harmony in processes and goals aligns efforts towards common objectives. Harmonism ensures that diversity of thought and resources are coordinated effectively, turning potential fragmentation into a cohesive framework for progress. [*Reference:* Covey, S.R. (2004). *The 8th Habit: From Effectiveness to Greatness*. Free Press.]

By embracing these qualities, societies can not only navigate through fragmentation but also transform it into an opportunity for deeper understanding and stronger unity. Collectively, these qualities create a model of leadership and community engagement that is both resilient and inclusive, steering towards a future marked by solidarity and cohesion.

We the People

We the people are traversing a turning point in the history of our species on Mother Earth. In light of this epic transformation, coalescing wisdom from the vast expanse of human learning and experience reveals perspectives that are emerging with promising insight and incalculable value.

Systemic and far-ranging examination of fragmentation invites deep consideration and unprecedented potential. This is especially engaging as we sense more clearly the intelligent nature of how fragmentation functions widely and impacts deeply the internal and external landscapes of the human in both the natural and constructed world. In fact, in every aspect of scientific inquiry this seemingly simple principle may be applied in expansive ways.

The key to achieving resonance and cohesion lies within us as a human race. The essence of human qualities—compassion humility, empathy, patience, respect, integrity, curiosity, forgiveness, and harmonism—embodies our innate ability to transcend differences and forge unity from diversity. They underscore the potential inherent in every individual and community to drive meaningful change. They remind us that the resources needed to bridge divides and build inclusive societies already exist within our collective human experience.

The interrelated nature of these qualities fosters an environment where humans can connect deeply and authentically. By leveraging these connections, we can address fragmentation with a holistic approach that appreciates varying perspectives and strengths. Emphasizing them helps develop resilience against divisive forces by promoting understanding and shared goals. When societies operate from a place of empathy and respect, they become more robust and adaptable in the face of adversity.

Despite the diversity of cultures, ideologies, and experiences, these qualities resonate as universal values that can be embraced worldwide. They provide common ground for dialogue and cooperation, serving as a foundation to address global challenges collaboratively. In recognizing and celebrating the diversity of human experiences and perspectives, these qualities enable us to achieve unity without demanding uniformity. They highlight how diversity enriches collective problem-solving and cultural depth, aligning disparate efforts towards an integrated whole.

Ultimately, these qualities invite us to reflect on our shared humanity. They challenge us to act from a place of kindness, curiosity, and integrity, encouraging us to build bridges rather than walls. Embracing these qualities collectively, we can create a world where the interconnectedness of our shared goals shines brighter than any divisiveness, where the destructive power of societal fragmentation is turned toward wholeness, harnessed to create a more cohesive and harmonious world.

e pluribus unum.

Afterword

In halls of power, great and vast,
Where voices echo from the past,
A push for speed, a push for gain,
Leaves values lost, and hearts in pain.

Compassion fades beneath the strain,
As hurried hands cut cords in vain,
With *empathy* cast to the breeze,
Voices plead, yet find no ease.

Humility, a distant call,
The shadow of ambition's sprawl,
Where *patience* is a whispered ghost,
And haste becomes the reigning host.

Respect, etched on the justice scale,
Now teeters in a restless gale,
While *integrity*, a solemn guide,
Fades off quietly to the side.

Curiosity yields to the known,
In echo chambers we've outgrown,
Forgiveness, a forgotten grace,
As judgment veils each tired face.

Harmonism is a quiet plea,
For unity in diversity,
Lost amid disjointed layers
Of policies and urgent prayers.

Might we find the strength to mend,
To weave these threads and comprehend,
That in our haste, we must not sever,
The bonds that make us whole forever.

-Virginia Ramos, JD, Spokane, WA

e pluribus unum

References

Adichie, D. N. (2013). *Americanah.* Alfred A. Knoph.

Adler, R. F., & Benbunan-Fich, R. (2012). Juggling on a high wire: Multitasking effects on performance. *International Journal of Human-Computer Studies, 70* (2), 156-168.

American Psychiatric Association (2013). *Diagnostic and Statistical Manual of Mental Disorders* (5th ed.). American Psychiatric Publishing

Amazeen, M. A. (2020). Journalistic interventions: The structural factors affecting the global emergence of fact-checking. *Journalism, 21*(1), 95-111, p. 1267.

Baer, W. S., & Parkinson, A. (2007). Cybersecurity and national policy. *Journal of Homeland Security and Emergency Management, 4* (2).

Bandura, A. (1997). *Self-Efficacy: The Exercise of Control.* W.W. Freeman and Company

Barth, J. R. (1991). *The Great Savings and Loan Debacle.* Washington, D.C.: American Enterprise Institute for Public Policy Research.

Benet-Martínez, V., Leu, J., Lee, F., & Morris, M. W. (2002). Negotiating biculturalism: Cultural frame switching in biculturals with oppositional vs. compatible cultural identities. *Journal of Cross-Cultural Psychology.*

Bennet, A. (2024). *Infinite Learning: Your Life, Your Choice.* MQIPress.

Bennet, A., & Bennet, D. (2004). *Organizational Survival in the New World: The Intelligent Complex Adaptive System.* Elsevier.

Bennet, A., & Turner, R. (2024). *Knowledge Capacities: Igniting Whole Thought.* MQIPress.

Bennet, A., & Turner, R. (2023). *Reblooming the Knowledge Movement: The Democratization of Organizations.* MQIPress.

Bennet, D. (2023). Systems and Complexity Thinking. In A. Bennet & R. Turner, *Reblooming the Knowledge Movement: The Democratization of Organizations.* MQIPress.

Bennet, D., Bennet, A., & Turner, R. (2023). *Unleashing the Human Mind: A Consilience Approach to Managing Self.* MQIPress.

Berger, W. (2014). *A More Beautiful Question: The Power of Inquiry to Spark Breakthrough Ideas.* Bloomsbury USA.

Bhabha, H. K. (1994). *The Location of Culture*. Routledge.

Blakely, E. J., & Snyder, M. G. (1997). *Fortress America: Gated Communities in the United States*. Brookings Institution Press.

Bolter, J. D., & Grusin, R. (2000). *Remediation: Understanding New Media* . MIT Press.

Brown. B. (2012). *Daring Greatly: How the Courage to be Vulnerable Transforms the Way we Live, Love, Parent, and Lead*. Gotham Books.

Burnes, B. (2004). Kurt Lewin and the Planned approach to Change: A Re-Appraisal. *Journal of Management Studies*.

Capra, F. (1996). *The Web of Life: A New Scientific Understanding of Living Systems*. Anchor Books.

Chatman, S. (1978). *Story and Discourse: Narrative Structure in Fiction and Film*. Cornell University Press.

Chorowicz, J. (2005). The East African rift system. *Journal of African Earth Sciences, 43* (1-3), 379-410.

Christopher, M. (2016). *Logistics and Supply Chain Management* (5ᵗʰ ed). Pearson.

Clampitt, P. G., DeKoch, R. J., & Cashman, T. (2000). A Strategy for Communicating About Uncertainty. *The Academy of Management Executive, 14*(4), 41-57.

Clark, A. (2016). "How a Water Crisis in Flint, Michigan Became a Nationwide Scandal." *The Guardian*.

Cloud, H. (2006). *Integrity: the Courage to Meet the Demands of Reality*. Harper Collins.

Coleman, J. S. (1990). *Foundations of Social Theory*. Harvard University Press.

Cooper, F. (2005). *Colonialism in Question: Theory, Knowledge, History*. University of California Press.

Covey, S.R. (2004). *The 8ᵗʰ Habit: From Effectiveness to Greatness*. Free Press.

Dalton, R. J. (2004).. Oxford University Press. *Democratic Challenges, Democratic Choices: The Erosion of Political Support in Advanced Industrial Democracies*.

Diamond, A. (2013). Executive Functions. *Annual Review of Psychology, 64* , 135-168.

Dicey, A.V. (first published in 1885). *Introduction to the Study of the Law of the Constitution*.

Dyson, M. E. (2006). *Come Hell or High Water: Hurricane Katrina and the Color of Disaster*. New York: Basic Books.

Eliasson, O. (2009). *Olafur Eliasson: Studio Olafur Eliasson*. Köln: Taschen.

Erikson, E. H. (1950). *Childhood and Society*. W.W. Norton & Company.

Erikson, E. H. (1968). *Identity, Youth and Crisis*. Norton.

Falola, T., & Heaton, M. M. (2008). *A History of Nigeria*. Cambridge University Press.

Fiorina, M. P., & Abrams, S. J. (2008). Political Polarization in the American Public. *Annual Review of Political Science, 11* , 563-588.

Frankl, V. E. (1959). *Man's Search for Meaning*. Beacon Press.

Fukuyama, F. (1995). *Trust: The Social Virtues and The Creation of Prosperity*. Free Press.

Fuller, L. L. (1964). *The Morality of Law*. Yale University Press.

Fulton, W., et al. (2001). *Who's your city?: How the creative economy is making where to live the most important decision of your life* . Basic Books.

Fung, A. (2015). Putting the public back into governance: The challenges of citizen participation and its future. Public Administration Review, 75(4), 513-522, p. 514.

Gardner, H. (1983). *Frames of Mind: The Theory of Multiple Intelligences*. Basic Books.

Gerken, H. K. (2017). Federalism as the new nationalism: An overview. *Yale Law Journal, 123*, 1889-1935.

Giddens, A. (1990). *The Consequences of Modernity*. Polity Press.

Gondry, M. (Director), & Kaufman, C. (Writer). (2004). *Eternal Sunshine of the Spotless Mind* [Motion picture]. United States: Focus Features.

Hardin, R. (2006). *Trust*. Polity.

Harindranath, R., & Sein, M. K. (2007). Revisiting the role of ICT in development. *Proceedings of the 9th International Conference on Social Implications of Computers in Developing Countries*.

Herman, J. L. (1992). *Trauma and Recovery: The Aftermath of Violence— From Domestic Abuse to Political Terror*. Basic Books.

Hess, E. D., & Ludwig, K. (2017). *Humility is the New Smart: Rethinking Excellence in the Smart Machine Age*. Berrett-Koehler Publishers.

Hetherington, M. J., & Rudolph, T. J. (2015). Why Washington won't work: Polarization, political trust, and the governing crisis. University of Chicago Press, p. 34.

Holland, J. H. (1992). *Adaptation in Natural and Artificial Systems: An Introductory Analysis with Applications to Biology, Control, and Artificial Intelligence.* MIT Press.

Hoofnagle, C. J., van der Sloot, B., & Borgesius, F. J. Z. (2019). The European Union general data protection regulation: What it is and what it means. *Information & Communications Technology Law, 28*(1), 65-98.

Inglehart, R., & Norris, P. (2017). Trump and the populist authoritarian parties: The silent revolution in reverse. *Perspectives on Politics, 15*(2), 443-454.

Iyengar, S., Sood, G., & Lelkes, Y. (2012). Affect, not ideology: A social identity perspective on polarization. *Public Opinion Quarterly, 76*(3), 405-431.

Kabat-Zinn, J. (1994). *Wherever You Go, There You Are: Mindfulness Meditation in Everyday Life.* Hachette Books.

Kahleer, M., & Lake, D. A. (Eds.) (2003). *Governance in a Global Economy: Political Authority in Transition.* Princeton University Press.

Kauffman, S. (1993). *The Origins of Order: Self-Organization and Selection in Evolution.* Oxford University Press.

Kegan, R., & Lahey, L. L. (2009). *Immunity to Change: How to Overcome It and Unlock the Potential in Yourself and Your Organization.* Harvard Business Press.

Kotter, J. P. (1996). *Leading Change.* Boston, MA: Harvard Business Review Press.

Kriesi, H., Grande, E., Lachat, R., Dolezal, M., Bornschier, S., & Frey, T. (2006). Globalization and the transformation of the national political space: Six European countries compared. *European Journal of Political Research, 45*(6), 921-956.

Krznaric, R. (2014). *Empathy: A Handbook for Revolution.* Random House.

Laurance, W. F., et al. (2001). The future of the Brazilian Amazon. *Science, 291* (5503), 438-439.

Levine, D. A., (2005). *Teaching Empathy: A Blueprint for Caring, Compassion, and Community.* Solution Tree.

Lewin, K. (1947). *Frontiers in Group Dynamics. Human Relations, 1*(1), 5–41.

Liiphart, A. (1999). *Patterns of Democracy: Government Forms and Performance in Thirty-Six Countries.* Yale University Press.

Lineham, M. M (1993). *Cognitive-behavioral treatment of Borderline Personality Disorder.* Guilford Press.

Lipset, S. M. (1960). *Political Man: The Social Bases of Politics*. Doubleday & Company, Inc.

Lotz, A. D. (2017). Portals: A treatise on internet-distributed television. *Media Industries Journal, 4* (2), 35-47.

Lucas, G. (Director). (1977). *Star Wars: Episode IV – A New Hope* [Motion picture]. Lucasfilm; 20th Century Fox.

Maeda, M., Jones, J., & McCormack, A. (Directors) (2003). *The Animatrix* [Animated short films]. Warner Brothers Pictures.

Marmot, M. (2004). *The Status Syndrome: How Social Standing Affects Our Health and Longevity*. Henry Holt and Company.

Margetts, H., John, P., Hale, S., & Yasseri, T. (2015). *Political Turbulence: How Social Media Shape Collective Action*. Princeton University Press.

Matthews, M. (2014, May 29). Why the VA's Imperfect Efficiency Fix Is My Favorite Newsweek Story of the Week. *Newsweek.*

Mayer, J. D., & Salovey, P. (1997). What is emotional intelligence? In P. Salovey & D. Sluyter (Eds.), *Emotional Development and Emotional Intelligence: Educational Implications* (pp. 3-31). Basic Books.

McCullough, M.E. (2008). *Beyond Revenge: The Evolution of the Forgiveness Instinct*. Jossey-Bass.

McDaniel, K. (2017). *The Fragmentation of the Soul*. Oxford.

Meshanko, P. (2013). *The Respect Effect: Using the Science of Neuroleadership to Inspire a More Loyal and Productive Workplace*. McGraw-Hill Education.

Mikulineer, M., & Shaver, P. R. (2007). *Attachment in Adulthood: Structure, Dynamics, and Change*. Guilford Press.

Newman, N., Dutton, W. H., & Blank, G. (2012). Social Media in the Changing Ecology of News: The Fourth and Fifth Estates in Britain. *International Journal of Internet Science, 7* (1), 6-22.

Nielsen, M. A., & Chuag, I.L. (2000). *Quantum Computation and Quantum Information*. Cambridge University Press.

Norris, P. (2011). *Democratic Deficit: Critical Citizens Revisited*. Cambridge University Press.

Orwell, G. (1949). *1984*. Secker & Warburg.

Paxton, R. O. (2005). *The Anatomy of Fascism*. Vintage.

Pert, C. B. (1997). *Molecules of Emotion: The Science Behind Mind-Body Medicine*. Scribner.

Piketty, T. (2014). *Capital in the Twenty-First Century*. Harvard University Press.

Piketty, T., & Saez, E. (2014). Inequality in the long run. *Science, 344*(6186), 838-843.

Prigogine, I., & Stenger, I. (2017). *Order Out of Chaos: Man's New Dialogues with Nature*. Verso.

Putnam, R. D. (2000). *Bowling Alone: The Collapse and Revival of American Community*. Simon & Schuster.

Putnam, R. D. (2007). E pluribus unum: Diversity and community in the twenty-first century. *Scandinavian Political Studies, 30*(2), 137-174.

Rothstein, B., & Teorell, J. (2008). What is quality of government? A theory of impartial government institutions. *Governance, 21*(2), 165-190.

Ryan, M. J. (2003). The Power of Patience: *How This Old-Fashioned Virtue Can Improve Your Life*. Conari Press.

Schein, E. H. (2010). *Organizational Culture and Leadership*. San Francisco, CA: Jossey-Bass.

Selman, D., & Leighton, P. (2010). *Punishment for Sale: Private Prisons, Big Business, and the Incarceration Binge*. Lanham, MD: Rowman & Littlefield Publishers.

Selman, D., & Leighton, P. (2010). *Punishment for Sale: Private Prisons, Big Business, and the Incarceration Binge*. Lanham, MD: Rowman & Littlefield Publishers.

Sidhu, R. S., et al. (2005). Impact of land fragmentation on productivity in Punjab: Paradigm shifts in land use. *Indian Journal of Agricultural Economics, 60* (4), 509.

Siegel, D. J. (2010). *Mindsight: The New Science of Personal Transformation*. Bantam.

Siegrist, J. (1996). Adverse health effects of high-effort/low-reward conditions. *Journal of Occupational Health Psychology, 1* (1), 27-41.

Sinardet, D. (2010). Belgium's "Impossible" Biculturalism: Between Cultural Diversity and Federalist Consensus. *Social Compass, 57* (2), 227-236.

Stiglitz, J. E. (2012). *The Price of Inequality: How Today's Divided Society Endangers Our Future*. W. W. Norton & Company.

Sunstein, C. R. (2009). *Going to Extremes: How Like Minds Unite and Divide*. Oxford University Press.

Sunstein, C. R. (2017). *Republic: Divided Democracy in the Age of Social Media*. Princeton University Press.

Tocqueville, A. de (2000). *Democracy in America.* Translated by Harvey C. Mansfield and Delba Winthrop. University of Chicago Press.

Tull, M. T., Stipelman, B. A., Salters-Pedneault, K., & Gratz, K. L. (2009).

Turner, R., & Bennet, A. (2024). *Knowledge Capacities: Cultivating Infinite Learning.* MQIPress.

Tykwer, T., Wachowski, L., & Wachowski, L. (Directors) (2012). *Cloud Atlas* [Motion picture]. Warner Brothers Pictures.

Tyler, T. (2020). Mobile App Development: iOS vs. Android. *Digital Development Journal.*

Uslaner, E. M. (2002). *The Moral Foundations of Trust.* Cambridge University Press.

Valkenburg, P. M., & Peter, J. (2011). Online Communication Among Adolescents: An Integrated Model of Its Attraction, Opportunities, and Risks. *Journal of Adolescent Health, 48*(2), 121-127.

Van Der Hart, O., Niijenhuis, E. R. S., & Steele, K. (2006). *The Haunted Self: Structural Dissociation and the Treatment of Chronic Traumatization.* W.W. Norton & Company.

Van Der Kolk, B. A. (2014). *The Body Keeps the Score: Brain, Mind, and Body in the Healing of Trauma.* Penguin Books.

Van Dijck, J., & Alinejad, D. (2020). Social media and trust in scientific expertise: Debating the Covid-19 pandemic. Social Media + Society, 6(4), 2056305120981057, p. 8.

Vosoughi, S., Roy, D., & Aral, S. (2018). The spread of true and false news online. *Science, 359*(6380), 1146-1151.

Wachowski, L., & Wachowski, L. (Directors) (1999). *The Matrix* [Motion picture]. Warner Brothers Pictures.

Weaver, K. (2000). "Ending Welfare as We Know It." *Brookings Institution.*

Whitacre, B. E., Gallardo, R., & Strover, S. (2014). Broadband's contribution to economic growth in rural areas: Moving towards a causal relationship. *Telecommunications Policy, 38* (11), 1011-1023.

Wintrobe, R. (1998). *The Political Economy of Dictatorship.* Cambridge University Press.

Zeidan, F., Johnson, S. K., Diamond, B. J., David, Z., & Goolkasian, P. (2010).

Zurek, W. H. (200). Decoherence, Einselection, and the Quantum Origins of the Classical. *Reviews of Modern Physics, 75(3), 715.*

About the Author

Alex Bennet is a Professor, Innovation and Knowledge Institute Southeast Asia (IKI-SEA), Bangkok University, and the Director of the Mountain Quest Institute, a research and retreat center located in the Allegheny Mountains of West Virginia. Through three quests—the quests for knowledge, consciousness and meaning—the Institute is dedicated to helping individuals achieve personal and professional growth, and organizations create and sustain high performance in a rapidly changing, uncertain, and increasingly complex world. Alex is the former Chief Knowledge Officer and Deputy CIO for Enterprise Integration of the U.S. Department of the Navy, having previously served as Acquisition Reform Executive and Standards Improvement Executive, and is recipient of the Distinguished Public Service Award, the highest civilian honor from the Secretary of the Navy. She has published hundreds of papers and journal articles, and authored, co-authored or edited over 40 books, primarily with her life partner, Dr. David Bennet, a nuclear physicist and neuroscientist, who recently transitioned. Together, the Drs. Bennet have spoken and taught around the world. In addition to the publications called out at the end of this book, publications emerging this year include *University of the Universe*, *C&C Thinking: Becoming Whole* (creative and critical thinking), *Contiguity: Entangled Living and Learning*, and *fRAGmentation: e Pluribus Unum*. Alex believes in the multidimensionality and interconnectedness of humanity as we move out of infancy into full consciousness. Contact her at alex@mountainquestinstitute.com

The Mountain Quest Research Center located in the Allegheny Mountains of West Virginia is a research, retreat, and learning center dedicated to helping individuals achieve personal and professional growth, and organizations create and sustain high performance in a rapidly changing, uncertain, and increasingly complex world. MQI has three quests: the Quest for Knowledge, the Quest for Consciousness, and the Quest for Meaning. MQI is scientific, humanistic, and spiritual and finds no contradiction in this blend.

Whole Thought:
The Rise of Human Intelligence **(2024)**

Alex Bennet and Robert Turner with Foreword by David Bennet

In tracing the arc of human progress, one can discern an underlying pattern steering the course of our intellectual evolution—a gradual but persistent gravitation towards what is now identified as Whole Thought. This paradigm does not represent a mere milestone, but rather signifies a shift, a transformation in the fabric of cognition brought into relief by the cumulative ascent of human intelligence.

Whole Thought

The Rise of Human Intelligence

Alex Bennet and Robert Turner
Mountain Quest Institute

The journey through the landscape of Whole Thought reveals an integrative approach to cognition that is as timely as it is timeless. It beckons us to rethink how we perceive, learn, and engage with the world and each other. Whole Thought is more than a theoretical concept; it is a call to action—a framework for living, learning, and leading in a manner that is reflective, inclusive, and deeply interconnected.

TRIBUTE

Deep appreciation for the life of

David Hughes Bennet

1934 – 2025

Author, Friend, Infinite Learner

Our capacity for knowledge is not a fixed quantity but a horizon ever-expanding. It is the reservoir from which we draw strength, the lens through which we view possibility, and the compass by which we navigate the future. It is the creation of the rise of human intelligence.

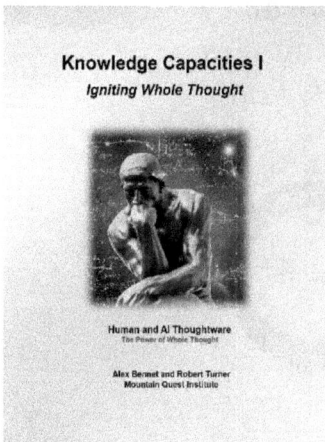

Knowledge Capacities I
Igniting Whole Thought

Human and AI Thoughtware
The Power of Whole Thought

Alex Bennet and Robert Turner
Mountain Quest Institute

Knowledge Capacities: Igniting Whole Thought—offering 40 Knowledge Capacities in support of Whole Thought, is open source and downloadable as a PDF from www.ResearchGate.edu , www.mountainquestinn.com (scroll to the bottom of the first page) and www.mqresearchcenter.com In cooperation with ROM Knowledge Management and for ease of copying and sharing, the Knowledge Capacities in the entire Whole Thought set are individually provided at www.kmrom.com/knowledge-capacities for download. By way of extension, Whole Thought and Knowledge Capacities are introductions to the new body of Human and AI Thoughtware.

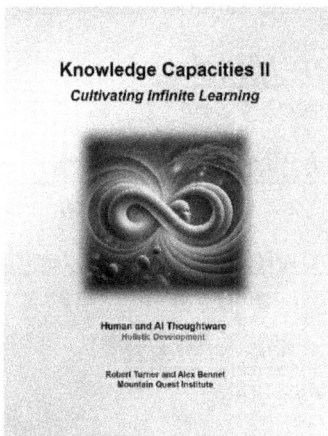

Knowledge Capacities II
Cultivating Infinite Learning

Human and AI Thoughtware
Holistic Development

Robert Turner and Alex Bennet
Mountain Quest Institute

Knowledge Capacities II: Cultivating Infinite Learning—offering 24 additional Knowledge Capacities in support of Whole Thought and cultivating infinite learning.

In today's dynamic and rapidly evolving environment, fostering capacity has become increasingly essential. Capacity refers to the broad potential or inherent ability of individuals and organizations to learn, adapt, and grow over time. It encompasses the fundamental ways of thinking, being, and acting that allow one to effectively engage with dynamic and complex environments. The broad and adaptive nature of capacities provides a robust foundation for continuous evolution and success.

Infinite Learning: Your Life, Your Choice (2025)
by Alex Bennet with Foreword by Vincent Ribiére

Infinite learning is the pulse of human existence, the essence that breathes life into our quest for understanding, innovation, and growth. Embracing infinite learning in pursuit of Whole Thought ensures that we do not merely exist but truly live, constantly expanding our horizons and discovering new potentials. *Living is learning; learning is living.*

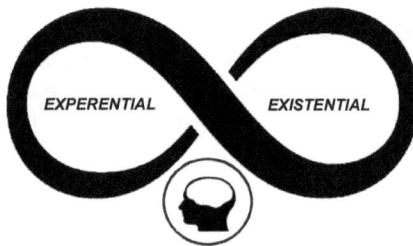

Infinite Learning
Your Life, Your Choice

Alex Bennet
Mountain Quest Institute

EXPERENTIAL ∞ EXISTENTIAL

Human and AI Thoughtware

Unleashing the Human Mind
A Consilience Approach to Managing Self

Whole Thought
The Rise of Human Intelligence

Infinite Learning
Your Life, Your Choice

Knowledge Capacities I
Igniting Whole Thought

Knowledge Capacities II
Cultivating Infinite Learning

Reblooming the Knowledge Movement
The Democratization of Organizations`

C&C Thinking: Becoming Whole (2025)
Critical and Creative

Alex Bennet and Robert Turner
with Foreword by Moria Levy

In an era marked by rapid technological advancement and constant change, the ability to think critically and creatively is more crucial than ever. As we look toward the future, it becomes evident that the traditional reliance on past patterns to predict and plan for what lies ahead is insufficient.

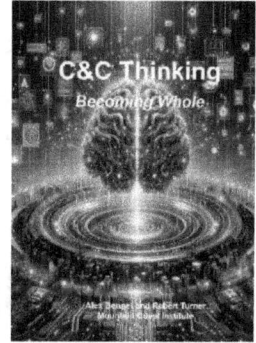

Contiguity: Entangled Living and Learning (2025)

Alex Bennet with Foreword by Chulatep Senivongse

Learning and living are contiguous experiences, with mind creating the subjective relationships that create the temporal and spatial relationships in our stories and memories. Our thoughts, sensations, and perceptions form the connected and cohesive experience of the contiguous mind. Embrace the entangled dance of living and learning, and discover the profound connections that define our shared existence.

fRAGmented: e Pluribus Unum (2025)

Alex Bennet

This is our world, a tapestry woven with threads of diversity and division. As we journey in this book through the complexities of our world, we critically explore fragmentation in the physical, holistic human, digital, narrative/art, and societal domains, and delve into the societal political fragmentation occurring today.

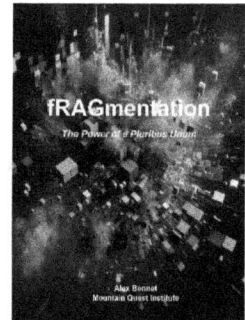

Recent Offerings from MQIPress

Reblooming the Knowledge Movement:
The Democratization of Organizations (2023)

Alex Bennet and Robert Turner with Foreword by Rory Chase and chapters contributed by Francisco Javier Carrillo, Mark Boyes, Florin Gaiseanu, Chulatep Senivongse, and Milton de Sousa

Reblooming unfolds on millennia of human challenges and advances. Now, at every level and at every reach across organizations, networks, and nations there is a new coalescing of democratization, intelligent learning, and capacity for surmounting complexity. With freedom of thought, freedom of expression, and freedom of association, ideas beget ideas. The emergent result is the rich globalization of knowledge and its close companion, innovation.

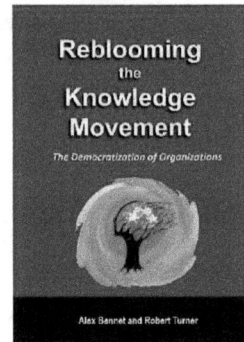

INside INnovation:
Looking from the Inside Out (2023)

Dr. Alex Bennet and Dr. Rajat Bais (Eds.) with Prologue by Dr. Leif Edvinsson and Foreword by Dr. Massimo Pregnolato

In addition to a collection of insightful innovation case studies, this book offers an unusual look at creativity and innovation from the inside out. Three innovators – a scientist, an organizational guru, and an artist – share the personal passions that have driven their success. "And, then, looking from the inside out, readers are provided the opportunity to evaluate their own organizations against the Most Innovative Knowledge Organization (MIKE) international study program and awards criteria, thus engaging their own innovative juices."

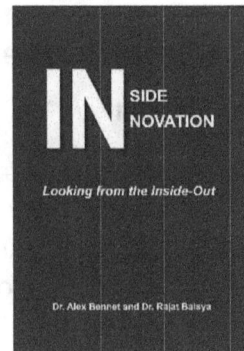

Unleashing the Human Mind:
A Consilience Approach to Managing Self (2022)

David Bennet, Alex Bennet, Robert Turner
with Foreword by Florin Gaiseanu

What does it mean to be human? Increasingly, we recognize that we are infinitely complex beings with immense emotional and spiritual, physical and mental capacities. Presiding over these human systems, our brain is a fully integrated, biological, and extraordinary organ that is preeminent in the known Universe. Its time has come. This book is grounded in the Intelligent Complex Adaptive Learning System (ICALS) theory based on over a decade of researching experiential learning through the expanding lens of neuroscience.

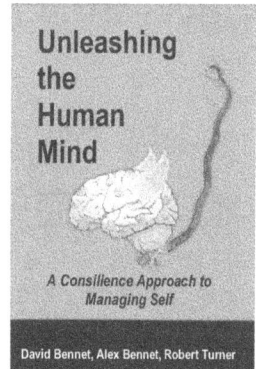

**Unleashing
the
Human
Mind**

*A Consilience Approach to
Managing Self*

David Bennet, Alex Bennet, Robert Turner

Review Bites from Around the World:

Once in a while, I am exposed to a work so profound that it literally causes a massive shift in my own thinking and beliefs ... I found myself riveted to each paragraph as I embarked on a journey that vastly deepened my understanding of the learning process.

-Duane Nickull, Author, Technologist, and Seeker of Higher Truth, Canada

Every now and then a book comes along that compels your spirit. In these times of uncertainty and even great danger for humanity, this book reminds us of what it means to be human, our infinite potential and innate ability to learn and to love.

-Dr. Milton deSousa, Associate Professor, Nova School of Business and Economics, Portugal

Very few people have the gift to integrate such complex ideas, especially those about learning ... this work can be likened to the Webb Telescope, which gives us more clarity into our mysteries.

-Michael Stankosky, DSc, Author, Philosopher, Professor, Editor-Emeritus, Member of the Academy of Scholars, USA

And the *Unleashing Field Guide: An OrgZoo Quest*

Alex Bennet, Robert Turner, Arthur Shelley, Jane Turner and Mark Boyes (Illustrator) (2022)

Arthur Shelley's beloved OrgZoo critters – the voices in our heads – join us in a learning quest up the mountain to unleash the human mind.

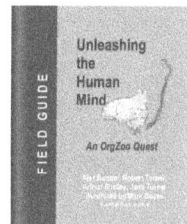

FIELD GUIDE

Unleashing
the
Human
Mind

An OrgZoo Quest

Alex Bennet, Robert Turner,
Arthur Shelley, Jane Turner
and Mark Boyes

Innovative Creativity: Creating with Innovation in Mind (2024)

Alex Bennet and Arthur Shelley with Charles Dhewa
Foreword by Robert Turner

More than ever, how do we release the Genie from the lamp? How do we tap the next level of creativity and innovation that we need here on Planet Earth? This groundbreaking work beckons us to deepen our innate creativity capacities in a new and expansive way to summon the genius within each of us.

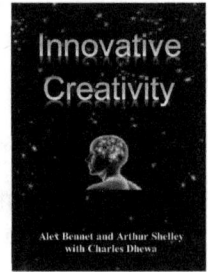

Innovative
Creativity

Alex Bennet and Arthur Shelley
with Charles Dhewa

Additional titles from MQIPress:

The Profundity and Bifurcation of Change: Parts I – V (2017; 2020)
Possibilities that are YOU! (a 22-volume conscious look book series) (2018)
The QUEST: Where the Mountains Meet the Library (2021)
Remembrance: Pathways to Expanded Learning (2020)
The Course of Knowledge: A 21st Century Theory (2015)
Decision-Making in The New Reality: Complexity, innovati (2013)
Expanding the Self: The Intelligent Complex Adaptive Learning System (2015)
Leading with the Future in Mind: Knowledge and Emergent Leadership (2015)
With Passion, We Live and Love: Research, Prose, Verse and Music (2021)
Playing in the Mind Field: Volume 1: Life in the Field (2023)

www.ingramcontent.com/pod-product-compliance
Lightning Source LLC
Chambersburg PA
CBHW070916270326
41927CB00011B/2593